Gifts from the Kitchen

Gifts from the Kitchen

ANNIE RIGG

PHOTOGRAPHY BY CATHERINE GRATWICKE

KYLE BOOKS

This paperback edition first published in Great Britain in 2015 by Kyle Books, an imprint of Kyle Cathie Ltd.
192–198 Vauxhall Bridge Road London, SW1V 1DX
www.kylebooks.com

ISBN: 978-0-85783-296-2

10 9 8 7 6 5 4 3 2 1

Text © 2010 Annie Rigg
Design © 2010 Kyle Cathie Limited

Photography © 2010 Catherine Gratwicke
pp. 10–11, 20–21, 43, 48
Laura Edwards

Editor Judith Hannam
Designer Rashna Mody Clark
Copy Editor Annie Lee
Food Stylist Annie Rigg
Prop Stylist Cynthia Inions
Proofreader Abi Waters
Index Hilary Bird
Production Gemma John

Annie Rigg is hereby identified as the author of this work in accordance with section 77 of the Copyright, Designs and Patents Act 1988.

A Cataloguing in Publication record for this title is available from the British Library.

Printed in Malaysia by Tien Wah Press

Contents

Introduction

Homemade gifts are those that are given with an extra ounce or two of love, a spoonful of originality and a jar-full of creativity. But homemade foodie gifts double those magic ingredients and tie them all up with a fancy ribbon.

There is a food gift for just about every occasion whether it be a birthday, Valentine's Day, Mother's Day or simply to welcome someone into their new home.

Some gifts aren't necessarily everyday food. Fortune cookies, each filled with a personal message, candy-striped bags of light-as-a-feather marshmallows and pastel-coloured Love Heart sugar cubes are purely for the joy and laughs that they'll bring and would be perfect for hen nights and weddings.

Receiving a box of homemade cookies is sure to brighten anyone's day and make the world seem a better place. So let no occasion pass unnoticed and imagine how fabulous it would be to give a box of the richest brownies or a tin of the stickiest, salted caramels for no particular reason, just simply because it's Friday, the sun is shining and you love someone. Any gift would be all the more special if you were able to grow or pick some of the ingredients yourself. A bumper crop of tomatoes can be turned into the most delicious chutney, an abundance of homegrown strawberries or a basket of windfall apples can be transformed into conserve, cordial or jelly. And no walk in the countryside is without its rewards, whether that be picking elderflower blossoms, juicy blackberries, damsons or sloes that can be infused in gin or turned into jams. For an extra touch, label your jars and preserves, not only with their contents but the day and location of the harvest.

Marmalade, seasonal jams and jellies can be made when the produce is at its very best and most plentiful. Squirrel the jars away in a dark cupboard or larder so that they are ready to bring out throughout the year or whenever the need arises.

Some gifts will need a little forward planning – flavoured vodkas or pickles need time to mature so if you're planning to give them away immediately, be sure to attach instructions for serving and storing.

It isn't just about what you make, it's about the presentation too. Look out for pretty vintage tins, boxes and baskets. Keep a good supply of gift tags and beautiful ribbons in all the colours of the rainbow so that every tray of cookies or candies can be dressed up to the nines. Collect jars, bottles and boxes throughout the year so that they are always on hand to be filled with your homemade delights.

IMAGINE HOW FABULOUS IT WOULD BE TO GIVE A BOX OF THE MOST COLOURFUL MACAROONS OR A TIN OF THE STICKIEST, SALTED CARAMELS FOR NO PARTICULAR REASON – JUST SIMPLY BECAUSE IT'S FRIDAY, THE SUN IS SHINING AND YOU LOVE SOMEONE.

SPRING

CHAPTER 1

Turkish Delight

Tip the sugar into a medium-sized pan and add the lemon juice and 300ml of water. Stir over a low heat to dissolve the sugar, then bring gently to the boil.

Mix the gelatine with 75g of the cornflour and 200ml water and add to the pan. Stir constantly until the gelatine has dissolved, then continue to simmer very gently for 20 minutes until thickened.

Mix together the remaining cornflour and the icing sugar. Lightly oil a 20cm square baking tin with a depth of 4–5cm and line it with clingfilm. Lightly dust the clingfilm with some of the cornflour mixture, tipping out the excess.

Remove the pan from the heat and set aside to cool. Add the rosewater, food-colouring and pistachios and pour the mixture into the tin. Spread level and leave to cool for at least 4 hours or until completely set before cutting into squares and dusting with the rest of the icing sugar and cornflour mixture.

 Stored in an airtight container, these will keep for about a week.

MAKES 20 PIECES

375g caster sugar

juice of 1 lemon

25g gelatine powder

100g cornflour

25g icing sugar

2–3 teaspoons rosewater

pink food-colouring paste

50g shelled unsalted pistachios, roughly chopped

sunflower oil, for brushing the tin

Homemade sweets and candies are always a pleasure to make and to receive. A box of sugar-dusted, rose-scented Turkish Delight is something we often associate with Christmas but would make a perfect Valentine's or Mother's Day gift packed into a box lined with waxed paper.

You could also try adding pure lemon extract and a drop of yellow food colour in place of the rosewater and pink colouring.

Coffee and Cardamom Toffee

There is something quite nostalgic and old-fashioned about toffee, but here it is given a contemporary twist with coffee and a hint of cardamom.

Brush the inside of a 17cm square baking tin with sunflower oil.

Place all the ingredients except the cardamom pods in a medium-sized pan and add 75ml water. Crack the cardamom pods using a pestle and mortar; remove the green husks and finely grind the little black seeds. Add to the pan and place over a low to medium heat. Stir to melt the butter and completely dissolve the sugars.

When the sugars have dissolved, raise the heat slightly and bring the mixture to the boil, stirring from time to time. Continue to cook steadily until the toffee registers 126°C/260°F (hard ball stage) on a sugar thermometer.

Remove the pan from the heat, give the toffee a quick whisk and pour into the greased baking tin. Leave to cool and harden before breaking into pieces and packaging in waxed paper.

Stored in an airtight container, the toffee will keep for about a week.

MAKES ABOUT 20 PIECES

sunflower oil, for brushing the tin
125g unsalted butter, diced
200g caster sugar
75g molasses sugar
2 rounded tablespoons golden syrup
2 teaspoons instant coffee granules
½ teaspoon ground cinnamon
pinch of salt
5–6 cardamom pods

Nougat with Cherries and Toasted Marcona Almonds

I have suggested using orange blossom-scented honey for this nougat but you could just as easily use any good-quality, fragrant variety. You could also swap the almonds for blanched, toasted hazelnuts and dried figs and cranberries for the cherries and apricots. Make the nougat the day before you plan on eating it so that it has plenty of time to harden and set.

Preheat the oven to 180°C/350°F/gas mark 4. Lightly grease a 15cm square tin with a depth of 5cm, and line the base and sides with a sheet of rice paper.

Lightly toast the almonds and pistachios in a baking tray in the oven until pale golden brown. Remove from the oven, allow to cool, then roughly chop. Cut the cherries in half, tip them into a sieve and rinse under cold running water. Dry well on kitchen paper. Roughly chop the dried apricots.

Place the honey, caster sugar and water in a medium pan. Set the pan over a medium heat, stirring occasionally until the sugar has dissolved. Increase the heat, bring the mixture to the boil, and continue to cook for about 10 minutes, until it reaches 164°C/327°F on a sugar thermometer. Remove the pan from the heat.

Whisk the egg white with a pinch of salt in a large heatproof bowl until it holds soft peaks – I recommend a free-standing mixer as it will make the process a lot easier. Continue to whisk while adding the hot honey caramel mixture in a steady stream. Keep whisking until the mixture stiffens, thickens and turns pale cream-coloured. Add the nuts and dried fruit and stir to combine. Spoon into the prepared tin and spread level. Press another sheet of rice paper on top and set aside to cool.

Once cold, tip the nougat out on to a board and cut into pieces.

Package in small quantities in transparent cellophane bags. Stored in an airtight container, the nougat will keep for 4–5 days.

MAKES ABOUT 20 SQUARES

2 large sheets of rice paper
100g blanched Marcona almonds
50g shelled, unsalted pistachios
100g natural coloured glacé cherries
50g dried apricots
175g clear orange blossom honey
300g caster sugar
2 tablespoons water
1 large egg white
pinch of salt

Pink and White Vanilla Marshmallows

Homemade marshmallows are the stuff of dreams! They are light as pink fluffy clouds, oh-so-sweet and with just a hint of pure vanilla extract. Cut into squares and package into pretty pink- and white-striped bags for hen nights and girly birthday parties.

Mix the icing sugar and cornflour in a small bowl. Lightly grease a 23cm square tin with a depth of about 5cm with a little sunflower oil and dust with the icing sugar and cornflour mix, tipping out and reserving the excess.

Measure 6 tablespoons of cold water into another small bowl, sprinkle over the gelatine and set aside.

Tip the sugar into a medium-sized pan, add 250ml water and the golden syrup and place the pan over a medium heat until the sugar has dissolved. Bring the mixture to the boil and continue to cook steadily until the syrup reaches 120°C/250°F on a sugar thermometer. Remove from the heat, add the sponged gelatine and stir until thoroughly combined and the gelatine has melted.

Place the egg whites in the bowl of an electric mixer fitted with a whisk attachment. Add a pinch of salt and whisk until the whites hold a stiff peak. Add the vanilla and the hot gelatine syrup in a steady stream and continue to whisk for a further 3–4 minutes, until the mixture will hold a ribbon trail when the beaters are lifted from the bowl.

Pour half the mixture into the prepared tin in an even layer. Add a tiny amount of pink food colouring paste to the remaining mixture and stir until evenly coloured. Pour the pink marshmallow over the white and leave to set (at least 2 hours).

Once the marshmallow has completely set, dust the work surface or a board with the remaining icing sugar and cornflour mixture. Carefully tip the marshmallow out on to the prepared board and cut into squares, using a sharp knife. Dust the individual marshmallows before packaging.

Package in striped paper bags.
Stored in an airtight box, the marshmallow will keep for 3 days.

MAKES ABOUT 30

1 tablespoon icing sugar
1 tablespoon cornflour
2 tablespoons powdered gelatine
400g granulated sugar
50g golden syrup
2 large egg whites
pinch of salt
1 teaspoon vanilla extract
pink food colouring paste

Lollipops

Use food-colouring pastes to tint these lollies whatever shade you desire. The colours are stronger, more varied, and each little pot seems to last for ever. If you can't get hold of a lolly mould, try setting the lollies in very well-greased round cutters or crumpet rings placed on a sheet of baking parchment. Remove the rings just before the lollies set solid, and firmly press a lolly stick into each one.
Or you could try making them free-form for a more homemade look!

Grease a 6-hole lolly mould with sunflower oil and line the bottom of each hole with a heart shape of greased baking parchment.

Tip the sugar and syrup into a small pan. Add the cream of tartar and 175ml of water. Set the pan over a gentle heat and warm slowly until the sugar has dissolved. Bring to a steady boil and continue to cook for about 10 minutes, until it reaches the 'hard crack' stage, 154°C/310°F on a sugar thermometer. Immediately remove from the heat and add the peppermint or lemon extract, swirling the pan to mix in evenly.

Pour roughly three-quarters of the mixture into a small warmed bowl and the rest into another. Add one of the food colourings to the larger quantity and the other to the smaller amount. Stir quickly until each mixture is evenly coloured.

Spoon the first mixture into the greased lolly moulds. Drizzle with the second mixture and lightly swirl the two together using a wooden skewer. Place a lolly stick into each lolly and leave to set until solid and completely cold before removing from the moulds.

Wrap individually in cellophane.
The lollies are best eaten on the day of making.

MAKES 6 LOLLIPOPS

sunflower oil, for greasing
300g granulated sugar
150g golden syrup
½ rounded teaspoon cream of tartar
2 teaspoons peppermint or lemon extract
2 contrasting food colouring pastes

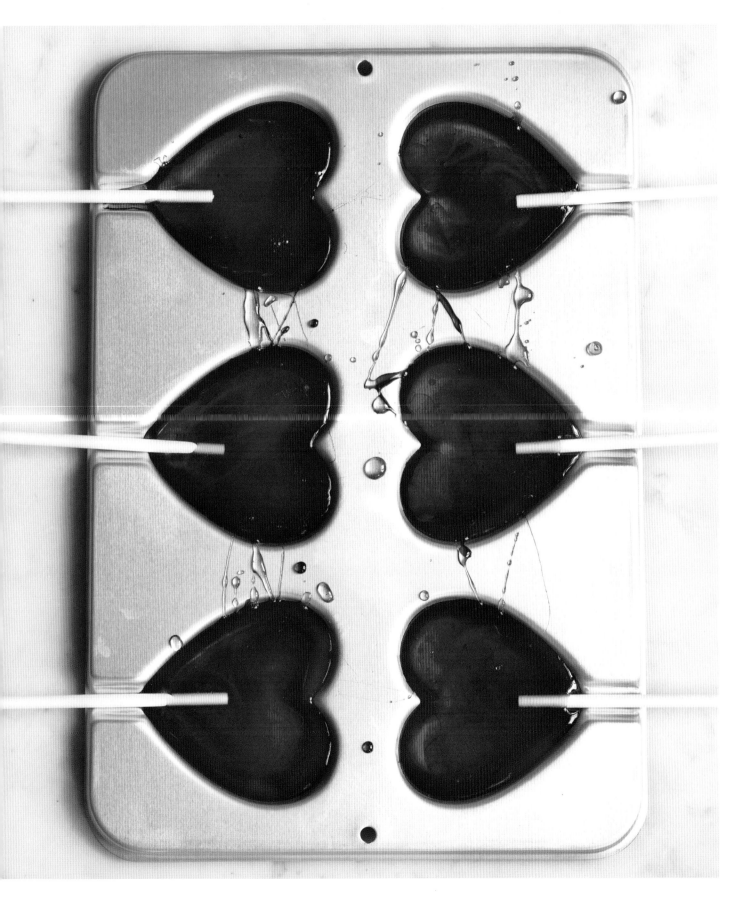

Macarons

Preheat the oven to 170°C/325°F/gas mark 3 and line 2 solid baking sheets with non-stick baking parchment.

Sift the icing sugar and ground almonds together into a bowl.

Place the egg whites in the bowl of a free-standing electric mixer fitted with a whisk attachment. Add the salt and whisk until the egg whites form soft peaks. Add the caster sugar a teaspoon at a time, whisking well after each addition. Continue whisking until the mixture is stiff and glossy.

Add the food colouring paste, using the point of a wooden skewer and mixing well to colour the mixture evenly. Fold the icing sugar and ground almonds into the mixture using a large metal spoon.

Fit a piping bag with a 1cm plain nozzle and pipe 5cm discs on to the baking parchment. Dampen the tip of your finger and gently flatten the top of any macaroons that are peaky, then give the tray a sharp tap on the work surface to knock out air bubbles. Set aside for 30 minutes to allow the mixture to settle, then bake on the middle shelf of the preheated oven for 9–10 minutes.

Remove from the oven and leave to cool on the tray.

Once completely cold, sandwich the macarons together with jam, cream, buttercream or ganache and serve.

MAKES ABOUT 20 MACARONS

150g icing sugar
75g ground almonds
2 large egg whites
pinch of salt
35g caster sugar
pink, green, yellow or lilac food colouring paste

Package up in brightly coloured boxes, tied with a ribbon. Once filled, the macarons can be kept in the fridge for a couple of days.

Making these delicate macarons can become seriously addictive – there is no end to the colour and flavour varieties you can create. Use food colouring pastes rather than the liquid variety to tint the macaron shells, a small pot will colour hundreds of macarons and the selection of colours now available is vast.

Sandwich the macarons with any number of fillings to match the colours – lemon curd, jam, buttercream or ganache are all perfect.

Chocolate and Cinnamon Swirl Meringues
and Pink Raspberry Swirl Meringues

Chocolate and Cinnamon Swirl Meringues

These meringues are big, pillowy sugary treats. The method of adding hot sugar to the egg whites means that once cooked the insides of the meringues stay chewy and marshmallowy while the outside is crisp.

Preheat the oven to 200°C/400°F/gas mark 6 and line a large, solid baking sheet with non-stick baking parchment.

Tip the sugar into a small roasting tin and place in the preheated oven for about 7 minutes, or until the sugar is hot to the touch. Meanwhile, place the egg whites in the bowl of a free-standing electric mixer fitted with a whisk attachment. Add the salt and whisk until frothy.

Turn the oven down to 110°C/225°F/gas mark ¼.

Quickly tip all the hot sugar on to the egg whites in one go and continue to whisk on high speed for 8–10 minutes, until the meringue mixture is very stiff, white and cold.

In a small bowl mix together the cocoa and cinnamon. Tip the cocoa mixture into the meringue and, using a large metal spoon, very lightly fold in, using two or three strokes. The trick is to keep the mixture quite marbled in appearance.

Spoon the mixture on to the prepared baking sheet in 4 or 6 equal-sized, peaky meringues. Cook on the middle shelf of the preheated oven for 1½–1¾ hours, or until dry and crisp. Remove from the oven and leave to cool on the baking sheet.

Package in cellophane bags tied with a contrasting ribbon and a label with serving instructions – the meringues are delicious eaten on their own or with lightly whipped double cream and maybe a scattering of raspberries. They will keep for 3–4 days in an airtight box.

MAKES 4–6 LARGE MERINGUES

300g caster sugar
4–5 large egg whites, weighing 150g
pinch of salt
2 tablespoons cocoa
1 teaspoon ground cinnamon

Pink Raspberry Swirl Meringues

Package these large clouds of raspberry swirled meringues in individual boxes lined with paper or in cellophane bags.
They are delicious eaten on their own or with a generous spoonful of softly whipped double cream and a handful of fresh raspberries.

MAKES 4–6 LARGE MERINGUES

300g caster sugar

4–5 large egg whites, weighing 150g

pinch of salt

½ teaspoon red food-colouring paste

2 tablespoons raspberry flavouring, optional

3–4 tablespoons (25g) freeze-dried raspberry crispies

FOR PISTACHIO AND COCONUT MERINGUES

50g desiccated coconut

50g unsalted and shelled pistachio nuts, finely chopped

Preheat the oven to 200°C/400°F/gas mark 6 and line a solid baking sheet with non-stick baking parchment.

Put the sugar into a small roasting tin and heat in the preheated oven for about 7 minutes, or until hot to the touch.

Place the egg whites and salt in the bowl of a free-standing electric mixer and whisk until light and foamy. Remove the hot sugar from the oven and turn the temperature down to 110°C/225°F/gas mark ¼. Quickly tip the sugar on to the egg whites and whisk on medium speed for 8–10 minutes, until the meringue is very stiff, white and cold.

Using a wooden skewer, dot the food colouring and drizzle the raspberry flavouring over the meringue mixture, then scatter over the raspberry crispies. Using a large metal spoon, very lightly fold in, using 3 or 4 strokes of the spoon, so that the meringue is marbled with pink.

Spoon the mixture on to the prepared baking sheet in 4–6 large peaky meringue shapes, and bake on the middle shelf of the preheated oven for 1½–1¾ hours, or until crisp. Remove from the oven and leave to cool on the baking sheet.

 Package in pretty boxes or cellophane bags. See serving suggestions opposite. They will keep for 3 days in an airtight box.

VARIATION:
Pistachio and Coconut Meringues

Make up the basic meringue, then add the desiccated coconut and the pistachios and fold in, using a large metal spoon. Divide the meringue into 4–6 even-sized portions and place on the baking sheet. Cook in the preheated oven for 1½–1¾ hours, then remove from the oven and leave to cool on the baking sheet.

Raspberry and Rose Chocolate Wafers

Line 2 large baking sheets with non-stick baking parchment.

Break the dark and white chocolate into pieces and melt separately in heatproof bowls set over pans of barely simmering water. Stir until smooth, remove from the heat and cool slightly. Spoon heaped teaspoonfuls of melted chocolate on to the prepared baking sheets, spreading the chocolate into discs with the back of the spoon. Scatter with the raspberry crispies, rose petals and rose chips or sugar sprinkles.

Set aside to cool and harden completely before removing from the parchment with a palette knife.

Stored in an airtight container, these will keep for 4–5 days.

MAKES ABOUT 24 WAFERS

150g best-quality dark chocolate (72% cocoa solids)

150g best-quality white chocolate

3–4 tablespoons freeze-dried raspberry crispies (approx. 25g)

3–4 tablespoons crystallized rose petals

3–4 tablespoons pink sugared rose chips or sugar sprinkles

A box of these chocolate
wafers would make an
ideal gift for Mother's Day
– they are easy enough
for little hands to make
as the only cooking
required is to melt
the chocolate.

Freeze-dried raspberries
are available on-line or
from good health food
shops. As an alternative
you could top the
chocolate wafers with
candied stem ginger or
chopped dried fruits
and nuts.

Chocolate and Hazelnut Madeleines

Light, buttery madeleines are almost begging to be served on the most delicate chinaware and at the most sophisticated tea party. They are cooked in special shell-shaped baking tins that are available in a variety of designs.

Preheat the oven to 180°C/350°F/gas mark 4.

Melt the butter either in a small saucepan or in a heatproof bowl in the microwave. Brush the insides of 2 madeleine tins with a little of the melted butter and then lightly dust them with plain flour, knocking out the excess flour by sharply tapping the tins on the work surface.

Sift the flour, baking powder, cocoa, ground hazelnuts and salt together into a large bowl.

Whisk the eggs, sugar and honey in a separate large bowl until they have doubled in volume, are very pale and thick and will hold a ribbon trail when the whisk is lifted from the mixture. Very gently fold in the sifted dry ingredients until only just incorporated. Add the remaining melted butter and gently fold this into the batter, trying not to knock out too much air from the mixture.

Spoon the mixture into the prepared tins, filling them three-quarters full. Bake on the middle shelf of the preheated oven for 10–12 minutes, until well risen and spongy.

Allow the madeleines to rest in the tins for 30 seconds, then turn them out on to wire racks and leave to cool.

MAKES ABOUT 20 MADELEINES

100g unsalted butter

100g plain flour, plus extra for dusting

½ teaspoon baking powder

1 tablespoon cocoa

25g ground hazelnuts

pinch of salt

2 large eggs

80g caster sugar

20g clear honey

icing sugar, to serve

Package in single layers in between parchment paper in pretty boxes or tins. They will keep for 2–3 days in an airtight box. Dust with icing sugar to serve.

Greek Honey Cookies

Try to use a deeply fragrant blossom honey for these pine nut-topped cookies. package in individual cellophane or paper bags or even empty cd or dvd envelopes which have a clever cellophane cut-out on the front, allowing the cookies to be seen.

MAKES ABOUT 20 COOKIES

250g plain flour

1 teaspoon baking powder

2 teaspoons bicarbonate of soda

1 teaspoon ground cinnamon

pinch of ground cloves

50g caster sugar

pinch of salt

125g unsalted butter, chilled and diced

finely grated zest of 1 orange

125g clear orange blossom or other fragrant honey

50g pine nuts

1 tablespoon clear honey, to finish

Preheat the oven to 180°C/350°F/gas mark 4 and line 2 solid baking sheets with non-stick baking parchment.

Sift the flour, baking powder, bicarbonate of soda, cinnamon, cloves, sugar and salt into a large mixing bowl. Add the butter and rub into the dry ingredients using the tips of your fingers. You can do this in a food processor if you like. Add the orange zest and mix well.

Warm the honey in a small pan until runny but not hot. Pour into the dry ingredients and mix well until smooth and thoroughly combined, and the dough comes together into a ball.

Break off dessertspoon-sized nuggets of the cookie dough, roll into balls and flatten slightly. Arrange on the prepared baking sheets, leaving plenty of space between them, and press a few pine nuts on to the top of each cookie. Bake on the middle shelf of the preheated oven for around 12 minutes, or until crisp and golden brown.

Leave on the baking sheets until cold, then lightly brush the tops of the warm cookies with a little honey and leave on the baking sheets until cold.

 Stored in airtight boxes or biscuit tins, they will keep for 4–5 days.

Candied Citrus Peel

This recipe makes enough candied peel to make up a number of small gifts. They are delicious eaten just as they are or you could take them to the next level and half dip them in very dark melted chocolate. Or for the keen baker they can be packaged into pretty screw-top glass jars to be used in baking.

Using a small, sharp knife, cut through the skins of the oranges, through the peel and pith and just down to the fruit, dividing the oranges into quarter segments. Carefully remove the peel still in the quarters, trying to leave as much of the pith attached to the skin as possible. Repeat with the grapefruit and lemon. Slice each piece of peel into strips no wider than 1 cm. Discard the fruit.

Place the strips in a large saucepan, cover with cold water and bring to the boil. Simmer for 2–3 minutes, then drain through a colander. Repeat this blanching twice more, using fresh water each time. This will remove any bitterness from the peel.

Wash and dry the saucepan. Place the sugar and 500ml water in the rinsed-out pan. Split the vanilla pod in half down its length, and add to the pan with the black peppercorns and cardamom pods. Bring slowly to the boil, stirring from time to time to dissolve the sugar. Add the blanched citrus peels and reduce the heat to a very gentle simmer. Continue to cook for around 2–3 hours, until the peels are very tender and become translucent. This time will vary depending on the variety of fruit used and how thickly you have cut the peels.

Using tongs, remove the peels from the syrup, draining off any excess, and put them on a large sheet of non-stick baking parchment in a single layer. Leave the candied peels to dry and for the sugar to crystallise – this can take anything up to 2–3 days, but will depend on the temperature of your kitchen.

The candied peels can be left as they are but are all the more delicious for being half coated in melted dark chocolate.

Toss the candied peels in caster sugar before packaging. In an airtight box or jar, they will keep for up to 1 month.

MAKES ENOUGH FOR 2–3 GIFTS

2 oranges
1 pink grapefruit
1 lemon
500g caster sugar
1 vanilla pod
½ teaspoon black peppercorns, lightly crushed
4 cardamom pods, lightly crushed
dark chocolate to coat (optional)

Vin d'Oranges

MAKES 2 X 500ml WINE BOTTLES

750ml fruity rosé wine
100ml vodka
100ml brandy
1 vanilla pod
1 large or 2 small cinnamon sticks
200g caster sugar
3 large Seville oranges
1 lemon

This recipe uses Seville oranges, which are only in season for a short time and are more commonly used to make marmalade. If you can't find Seville or bitter oranges for this recipe you could use ordinary oranges and perhaps slightly less sugar. Decant the Vin d'Oranges into pretty bottles and serve chilled.

Pour the wine, vodka and brandy into a large (3 litre), sterilised kilner jar (see page 168). Split the vanilla pod in half and add to the jar with the cinnamon and sugar. Seal the jar securely and give it a good shake to dissolve the sugar into the alcohol.

Wash the oranges and the lemon and pat dry on kitchen paper. Cut the fruit in half and then into 5mm thick slices. Add the sliced oranges and lemon to the jar, seal and shake again.

Leave the vin d'oranges in the fridge for about 1 month, giving it a good shake every now and then. Strain, decant into pretty sterilised bottles (see page 168) and label.

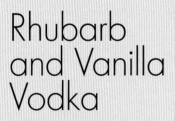 It will keep, decanted, in the fridge, for 2–3 months.

Rhubarb and Vanilla Vodka

MAKES 1 LARGE BOTTLE

600g rhubarb, trimmed weight
1 vanilla pod
250g caster sugar
1 x 70cl bottle of good-quality vodka

I can highly recommend serving this vodka ice-cold as a martini – though don't be fooled by it's innocent-looking and sweet-tasting pinkness...

For this recipe you really must use the forced Barbie-pink rhubarb as this is what gives the finished vodka its delicate blush colour.

Rinse the rhubarb under cold running water, cut into 2cm lengths and place in a shallow pan. Split the vanilla pod in half down its length. Using the point of a sharp knife, scrape the seeds out of each half and add the seeds and pods to the pan along with the caster sugar.

Stir over a low heat until the sugar has dissolved, then continue to cook for about 3–5 minutes, until the rhubarb is just starting to soften and release its beautiful pink juice. Remove the pan from the heat and leave to cool.

Spoon the contents of the pan into a sterilised 2 litre kilner jar (see page 168). Pour over the vodka, stir well and seal the jar securely. Leave in the bridge for about 2 months, shaking the jar once a week, until the vodka is deliciously pink and scented with the rhubarb and vanilla. Strain through muslin and decant into pretty bottles.

It will keep for up to 3 months in the fridge.

SUMMER

CHAPTER 2

Apple and Mint Jelly

How wonderful would it be if you were able to use home-grown apples and garden mint for this scrumptious jelly? I find jellies easier to make in smaller batches and so have suggested bottling this in little jars, and besides it's too special for every day. Perfect with roast lamb.

Wash the apples and cut out any large bruises. Quarter the unpeeled apples and cut into chunks, but do not remove the cores and pips. Put them into a preserving pan or large saucepan, add 600ml water, cover the pan and cook gently until the apple chunks have fallen apart and are very soft.

Tip the contents of the pan into a jelly bag, suspend over a large bowl and leave the juice to slowly drip through. This will take at least 4 hours. Do not be tempted to push or prod the apples or the resulting juice will be cloudy.

Pour the juice into a measuring jug and make a note of the amount. For every 600ml of juice you will need 450g of granulated sugar. Pour the juice back into a clean pan, then add the sugar and heat gently until it has dissolved. Bring to the boil and cook for a couple of minutes, then add the vinegar and salt. Continue to cook at a steady boil until setting point has been reached (see page 168) for about 10 minutes, removing any scum from the surface with a large spoon.

Remove the pan from the heat and leave to cool for 5 minutes. Add the chopped mint and stir to distribute it evenly throughout the jelly. Pour the jelly into small, sterilised jars (see page 168) and seal immediately.

Label the jars once completely cold. Jelly will keep for months if stored unopened in a cool, dark cupboard or larder. Once opened, store in the fridge and use within 1 month.

MAKES 4 SMALL JARS

1kg Bramley apples
approx. 450g granulated sugar
4 tablespoons white wine vinegar
½ teaspoon salt
4–5 tablespoons finely chopped fresh mint

Strawberry and Rose Petal Cordial

If you're lucky (and green fingered) enough to grow old-fashioned scented roses, then spare a handful or two of the petals to be added to this cordial. Store the cordial in the fridge and serve diluted to taste with sparkling mineral or soda water and plenty of ice. Or pour a generous glug over vanilla ice cream and add a handful of sliced summer berries for a scrumptious ice cream sundae.

Put the sugar into a medium-sized pan and add 300ml of cold water. Using a vegetable peeler, pare the zest from the lemon in strips and add to the pan along with the squeezed lemon juice. Set the pan over a low to medium heat, stirring occasionally to dissolve the sugar, then bring to the boil and simmer for 2 minutes.

Remove the pan from the heat and add the strawberries, rose petals and citric acid. Gently crush the berries in the pan with the back of a spoon. Leave the fruit and petals to steep in the syrup for about 4 hours.

Strain the cordial through a fine sieve or muslin, then pour into sterilised bottles (see page 168), seal and label. Store in the fridge until ready to serve.

It will keep, in the fridge, for a couple of weeks.

MAKES ABOUT 500ml

300g caster sugar

juice and zest of 1 unwaxed lemon

500g ripe hulled strawberries, quartered

2 handfuls of fragrant, unsprayed rose petals, washed

1 teaspoon citric acid

Summer Berry Vodka

Serve this berry-infused vodka in cocktails or ice
cold in little shot glasses. You could also try adding a
dash to Champagne as an alternative Kir Royale.

Place the raspberries, strawberries, lemon zest and caster sugar in a
large bowl and lightly crush with the back of a wooden spoon or fork.
Add the vanilla pod, mix well and leave to one side for about 2 hours,
until the sugar has dissolved and the fruit starts to become really juicy.

Spoon the contents of the bowl into a large sterilised kilner jar (see page
168) and pour in the vodka. Mix well and chill for 1 week or until needed
(up to about a month).

Strain the vodka through a fine sieve or muslin, and decant into pretty
sterilised bottles.

It will keep, in the fridge, for up to 2 months.

MAKES ABOUT 800ml

350g raspberries

**350g strawberries, hulled and
quartered**

pared zest of 1 unwaxed lemon

200g caster sugar

1 vanilla pod, halved

**1 x 70cl bottle of good-quality
vodka**

There's nothing quite like homemade lemon curd. And when you add passionfruit to the mix, you're on to something really special. Serve it with freshly baked scones (or shortcakes), hot buttered English muffins, or spread between vanilla sponge cake layers with lashings of whipped cream and fresh berries.

Lemon and Passionfruit Curd

MAKES 4 SMALL JARS

4 large eggs

125g unsalted butter, cubed

225g caster sugar

zest and juice of 3 unwaxed lemons

seeds and pulp of 2 passionfruit

Beat the eggs and strain into a medium-sized heatproof bowl. Add the remaining ingredients and place the bowl over a pan of simmering water. Do not allow the bottom of the bowl to come into contact with the water or the heat will scramble the eggs.

Stir the mixture constantly until it reaches the consistency of very thick custard. Remove from the heat and stand the bowl in a sink of cold water to speed up the cooling process, stirring occasionally until cold.

Pour into sterilised jars (see page 168), cover and store in the fridge until needed.

 It will keep, in the fridge, for up to 1 week.

Hot Chilli Jelly

I would suggest making this fiery little number in small batches — not only does a little go a long way, but it's a true labour of love chopping those chillies.

MAKES 3–4 SMALL JARS

750g Bramley apples

approx. 225g granulated sugar

½ teaspoon salt

2 tablespoons white wine vinegar

4–5 red chillies, deseeded

1 red pepper

Wash the apples and cut into chunks (peel, core and pips included). Tip the apple chunks into a pan, add 450ml water, cover and cook over a low to medium heat until the apples are really tender and have fallen apart. Scoop the contents of the pan into a jelly bag suspended over a bowl, and leave for at least 4 hours or overnight to allow the apple juice to slowly drip through. Do not be tempted to push the apples through the bag or the resulting jelly will be cloudy.

The next day, pour the strained juice into a measuring jug and make a note of the quantity. Pour the juice back into a clean pan and add 450g of granulated sugar per 600ml of apple juice. Put the pan over a low heat and stir to dissolve the sugar, then bring to the boil. Simmer for a couple of minutes, then add the salt and vinegar.

Continue to cook at a steady boil until setting point is reached (see page 168), which will most likely take about 10 minutes.

While the jelly is boiling, prepare the chillies and red pepper. Deseed and roughly chop them and blend quickly in a food processor until finely chopped. Once the jelly reaches setting point, add the chopped chillies and pepper to the pan and continue to cook for a further 2 minutes.

Take the pan off the heat and leave the jelly to settle for 2 minutes before pouring into small, sterilised jars (see page 168). Seal immediately and leave to cool completely before labelling.

This jelly can be used immediately as it's not like a chutney where the vinegar and spices need to mellow. Store in a cool, dark cupboard or larder. Once opened, store in the fridge and use within 1 month

Redcurrant Curd

Look out for little punnets of jewel-like redcurrants in the greengrocers during the summer months and try this as an alternative to lemon curd.

Strip the redcurrants from their stalks, using a fork. Place in a small pan with a splash of water and cook over a low heat for about 5 minutes, until the currants are very soft. Push the fruit and juice through a nylon sieve into a bowl.

Return the redcurrant purée to a clean pan and add the caster sugar (varying the amount depending on how sweet the purée is) and the butter. Stir over a low heat until the butter has melted and the sugar has dissolved.

Beat the whole egg and yolks together in a small bowl, then whisk in 2–3 tablespoons of the hot redcurrant mixture. Return the whole mixture to the pan. Stirring constantly, cook over a low heat for about 2 minutes, until thickened. Do not allow the curd to boil or the eggs will scramble.

Strain the curd into a jug, then pour into dry sterilised jars (see page 168) and seal.

Keep in the fridge and use within 1 week. Attach a label to the jar with serving suggestions such as spooning the curd in between buttery layers of vanilla-scented cake and lightly whipped double cream or spreading into miniature sweet pastry cases and topping with a pillow of meringue.

MAKES 2 JARS

300g redcurrants
100–125g caster sugar
25g unsalted butter
1 large egg
2 large egg yolks

Strawberry and Vanilla Conserve

A recipe for the height of summer when soft fruit is at its best, perfectly ripe and intensely sweet. Conserve has a slightly softer set than jam as the fruit remains whole or in large pieces and for this reason it really is important to use small, ripe strawberries. The result will be a pot of the most intense strawberry flavour with a vibrant red colour. The hint of vanilla seeds will enhance the strawberry flavour without overpowering it. I'm thinking scones, clotted cream and lazy, sunny afternoons in the garden...

Tip the sugar into a preserving pan or other large pan. Add the lemon juice and 2 tablespoons of water. Split the vanilla pod in half lengthways, then using the tip of a small knife scrape out the little black seeds and add the pod and seeds to the pan. Set over a low heat and stir from time to time until the sugar has dissolved.

Remove the pan from the heat, add the strawberries and stir gently to coat in the hot syrup. Leave to stand for 30–60 minutes, to allow the fruit to soften and release its juice into the syrup.

Return the pan to a medium heat and cook at a steady boil, without stirring, for about 10 minutes, or until the conserve reaches setting point (see page 168).

Remove the pan from the heat, discard the vanilla pod and leave the conserve to cool in the pan for about 10 minutes as this ensures that the strawberries are evenly distributed throughout once the conserve is bottled.

Carefully spoon into sterilised jars (see page 168) and seal immediately. Leave to cool completely before labelling.

This will keep for months, unopened, in a cool, dark cupboard or larder and, once opened, for up to 1 month in the fridge.

MAKES 3–4 SMALL JARS
450g preserving sugar
juice of 1 lemon
1 vanilla pod
550g small ripe strawberries, hulled

Cherry Jam

MAKES 3 X 450g JARS

750g ripe cherries
600g preserving sugar
juice of ½ a lemon

This is one of my favourite homemade jams. The cherries are pitted and kept whole which make the jam somehow more indulgent, especially when spooned onto toasted buttered crumpets or homemade English muffins.

Remove the stones from the cherries, using a cherry pitter if you have one. Place the cherries in a large, solid-based saucepan or preserving pan and add 3–4 tablespoons water. Set the pan over a low to medium heat and cook gently until the cherries are very soft.

Add the sugar and lemon juice and stir gently until the sugar has dissolved. Increase the heat slightly and boil steadily for 20 minutes, or until setting point has been reached (see page 168).

Remove the pan from the heat and leave the jam to rest for 10–15 minutes before spooning into sterilised jars (see page 168). Resting the jam will cool it sufficiently so that the cherries are suspended rather than sinking to the bottom of the jars. Cover immediately and leave the jam to cool completely before labelling.

 This will keep for months, unopened, in a cool, dark cupboard or larder and, once opened, for up to 1 month in the fridge.

Seedless Blackcurrant Jam

MAKES 2 X 450g JARS

500g blackcurrants
450g preserving sugar

Although this doesn't make a vast quantity of jam, the end result is so intense that a small teaspoonful will instantly transport you to high summer. Sublime on hot buttered toast!

Place the blackcurrants in a large pan with 250ml water. Bring slowly to the boil, then reduce the heat and simmer gently for about 3 minutes, to allow the fruit to soften and burst.

Press the fruit and juice though a nylon sieve set over a bowl to extract all the pulp and remove the seeds.

Return the blackcurrant pulp to the clean pan and add the preserving sugar. Stir constantly over a low heat until the sugar has dissolved, then increase the heat and boil rapidly until setting point has been reached (see page 168) – this will take no more than 10 minutes.

Pour the jam into sterilised jars (see page 168) and seal immediately.

This will keep for months, unopened, in a cool, dark cupboard or larder and, once opened, for up to 1 month in the fridge.

Raspberry and Passionfruit Pastilles

Cut these pastilles into small squares, toss in caster sugar and pack into pretty glass candy jars tied with ribbons and a gift tag.
One batch of this recipe will make enough pastilles to fill a couple of jars making two gifts at once.

Try using a small heart-shaped cutter to stamp out the pastilles, toss in sugar and package into little bags or boxes as wedding favours or Valentines gifts. Any off-cuts are a little gift to yourself.

Lightly oil a 17cm square baking tin and line with non-stick baking parchment.

Tip the raspberries into a solid-bottomed shallow pan. Halve the passionfruit and scoop the seeds and juice into the pan. Add the lemon juice, cover the pan and cook over a medium heat until the raspberries have softened and cooked down to a pulp.

Remove from the heat and push the fruit through a fine nylon sieve into a bowl. Weigh the resulting purée and return it to a clean pan. Add an equal quantity of preserving sugar and stir over a low to medium heat until it has dissolved. Continue to cook for about 30 minutes, stirring frequently with a wooden spoon, until the purée has reduced and thickened considerably to the consistency of jam and reached setting point (see page 168).

Use a rubber spatula to scoop the purée into the prepared tin and leave to set for at least 6 hours or overnight.

Cover a baking sheet or tray with a sheet of non-stick baking parchment sprinkled liberally with caster sugar. Flip the pastille mixture out of the tin and on to the sugar-covered paper, and carefully peel off the backing paper. Cut into pastilles and toss in the caster sugar to coat completely. Leave to dry for 1 hour before packaging.

Store in an airtight jar. These pastilles will keep for 4–5 days.

MAKES 20 PIECES

400g raspberries
3 passionfruit
juice of ¼ lemon
approx. 300–400g preserving sugar with added pectin
caster sugar, to serve

Love Heart Sugar Cubes

Not really cubes at all. These little sugar hearts would make the perfect gift for valentines, a hen night or as a wedding favour. You could tint the sugar almost any colour imaginable but pale, pastel shades are more elegant when teamed with vintage tea cups. Why stop at love heart sugar cubes?

Look out for small star or simple flower shaped cutters to experiment with.

MAKES LOTS!

250g caster sugar
food colouring pastes
(pink and other
pastel colours)

Line 2 baking sheets with non-stick baking parchment. Put the sugar into a bowl, add 1–2 tablespoons cold water and stir thoroughly until the sugar takes on the texture of damp sand, the kind you'd use to make sandcastles, adding more water or sugar to achieve the correct texture.

Tip half the mixture on to one of the baking sheets and press firmly to a thickness of 1cm. Using a small heart-shaped cookie cutter, stamp out shapes, one at a time. Using your fingers, gently push each sugar heart out of the cutter and on to the second baking sheet. Repeat until you have used up all the white sugar mixture.

Using a cocktail stick, add a tiny amount of pink food colouring paste to the remaining mixture and stir until combined. Stamp out more hearts in the same way. Leave to dry overnight.

Package into pretty boxes. They will keep for up to 1 month.

Cherry Tomato and Sweet Chilli Jam

A number of recipes in this book would be perfect to make and give together – this is one such recipe. I can't get enough of this sweet, spicy relish spread on top of Oatmeal Biscuits for Cheese (page 120) with some tangy marinated goats cheese (page 58) crumbled on top.

MAKES 3–4 X 250g JARS

2 onions

750g ripe cherry tomatoes, halved

2 fat cloves of garlic, crushed

2 large mild red chillies, deseeded and finely chopped

5cm piece of fresh ginger, grated

2 teaspoons cumin seeds

2 teaspoons coriander seeds

250ml white wine vinegar

300g soft light brown sugar

2 teaspoons fish sauce (or soy sauce if making this for vegetarians)

Peel and finely chop the onions and place in a wide saucepan with the tomatoes, garlic, chillies and ginger.

Toast the cumin and coriander seeds in a small, dry frying pan over a low heat for 1 minute until aromatic, then remove from the pan and grind in a pestle and mortar. Add to the saucepan along with the wine vinegar and sugar.

Cook over a low to medium heat until the sugar has dissolved. Bring to the boil, then reduce the heat to a simmer and continue to cook until the mixture has reduced to a syrupy jam consistency, stirring from time to time. Add the fish sauce (or soy sauce) and cook for a further couple of minutes before spooning into small sterilised jars (see page 168). Seal the jars while hot and allow to cool completely before labelling and storing.

 This will keep for months, unopened, in a cool, dark cupboard or larder and, once opened, for up to 1 month in the fridge.

Spice Mix

With a jar of this spice mix, a couple of fabulous steaks, some spiced plum Barbecue Sauce (page 56) and a bottle of Chilli Vodka (page 167), you could find yourself the number one guest at any summer barbecue.

Lightly bruise and crack the cardamom pods using a pestle and mortar or by giving them a sharp tap with a rolling pin. Remove and discard the papery green outer husks and tip the little black seeds into a dry frying pan. Add the peppercorns and the cumin, coriander and fennel seeds. Toast the spices in a dry frying pan over a low heat for about 2–3 minutes, until they start to smell very aromatic and begin to brown slightly.

Immediately tip the toasted seeds into the mortar, add the crushed chilli flakes and finely grind with the pestle. Add the remaining ingredients to the mortar and mix to combine.

Scoop the spice mix into a sterilised jar (see page 168), seal and label with barbecuing instructions.

Sprinkle spice mix over steaks, chicken or veggies and leave to marinade before barbecuing. Stored in a screwtop jar, it will keep for up to 1 month.

MAKES 1 X REGULAR JAM JAR

6 cardamom pods
2 teaspoons black peppercorns
4 teaspoons cumin seeds
4 teaspoons coriander seeds
4 teaspoons fennel seeds
1 teaspoon crushed dried red chilli flakes
2 teaspoons dried oregano
1 teaspoon paprika
2 teaspoons sea salt
1 rounded teaspoon dry mustard powder
3–4 teaspoons caster sugar

Spiced Plum Sauce for Barbecues

Not only would this sauce be the thing to serve alongside chargrilled bangers and burgers but it's not half-bad when basted over barbecued ribs and chicken.

Wash the plums, cut them into quarters and remove the stones. Peel and chop the onions and tip into a preserving pan with the plums. Add the garlic and ginger and put all the spices in a muslin bag and also add to the pan.

Add the sugar and vinegar and set the pan over a medium heat, stirring from time to time until the sugar has dissolved. Bring the mixture slowly to the boil, then reduce to a gentle simmer and continue to cook until the plums and onions are very soft. This can take about 1 hour.

Remove the muslin bag of spices and tip the sauce into a mouli-légumes set over a clean pan. Stir it through a mouli to remove any tough plum skins. Place the pan over a low to medium heat and continue to cook for about 10 minutes, until thickened to the consistency of tomato ketchup.

Taste, and add the soy sauce and a little more sugar if needed to balance the flavours.

Carefully pour the sauce into sterilised jars or bottles (see page 168) and seal. Leave to cool before labelling.

Store for months unopened in a cool, dark cupboard or larder. Once opened, store in the fridge and use within 1 month.

MAKES 4 X 450g JARS

1.5kg red or purple plums
2 small onions
2 fat cloves of garlic, peeled and sliced
5cm piece of fresh ginger, grated
1 teaspoon black peppercorns
1 small cinnamon stick
4 allspice berries
2 teaspoons sea salt
2 star anise
5 whole cloves
300g soft light brown sugar
500ml white wine vinegar
1–2 tablespoons soy sauce

Scandinavian-Style Crispbread

I like to use a combination of flours for these crispbreads – rye, wholemeal, spelt and maybe even some white bread flour all work well. Traditionally the crispbreads would be rolled with a special knobbly rolling pin before baking, but pricking them all over with a fork or pressing the fine side of a grater over the surface of each one works just as well.

MAKES 3 OR 4 X 250g JARS

1 teaspoon active dried yeast

1 teaspoon clear honey

500g rye flour or a combination of flours (see above), plus extra for rolling out

1 teaspoon sea salt flakes, plus a little extra

1 teaspoon caraway seeds, lightly crushed

1 teaspoon poppy seeds

1 teaspoon sesame seeds

Whisk the yeast and honey into 300–325ml warm water in a measuring jug and leave in a warm place for around 5 minutes until a light, yeasty foam forms on top of the water.

Tip the flour into a large bowl, stir in the salt, caraway, poppy and sesame seeds and make a well in the middle of the dry ingredients. Pour the yeasty water into the bowl and mix with a wooden spoon until the mixture comes together into a ball. Turn out onto a clean work surface and knead lightly for about 3–4 minutes until smooth. Shape into a ball, return the dough to the bowl, cover with cling film and leave to prove in a warm place for 1 hour.

Preheat the oven to 190°C/375°F/gas mark 5.

Lightly dust the work surface with flour and divide the dough into 12–16 even-sized balls. Roll each piece out as thinly as possible and, using a side plate as a guide, cut each piece into a neat disc. Using a 4cm round cutter, stamp out a small disc from the middle of each piece, prick the dough with a fork or press the surface with a grater, scatter with a little more sea salt and bake in batches on the middle shelf of the preheated oven for around 10 minutes until crisp and golden, turning the crispbreads over halfway through the baking time.

Cool completely before packaging and tie a ribbon through the hole.

These crispbreads would be delicious with gravad lax (page 164) or pork rillettes (page 64) or simply served with soft herby cheese. Stored in an airtight box, they will keep for a couple of weeks.

Marinated Goat's Cheese

Use the small young Crottin goat's cheeses for this recipe and some fine quality, fruity olive oil for the marinade to make this really special. I have suggested using fresh oregano but you could just as easily use a couple of sprigs or rosemary or thyme. A jar of these cheeses would make a tasty addition to any picnic hamper or summer cheese board.

Pack the cheeses into a sterilised, wide-necked storage jar (see page 168), and add the bay leaf and oregano leaves. Cut the chilli in half through the stalk and pare 2 strips of zest from the lemon. Arrange the chilli and lemon zest around the cheeses. Add the fennel seeds and garlic cloves, and pour over extra virgin olive oil so that the cheeses are completely covered. Seal the jar and chill. Bring back to room temperature to serve.

Store in the fridge for up to 1 week until needed and then drain and eat with some fabulous bread, crumbled into salads or grilled on slices of baguette with a good spoonful of Tomato Chutney (page 85).

MAKES 1 LARGE JAR

4 young Crottin goat's cheeses

1 bay leaf

½ tablespoon fresh oregano leaves

1 red bird's-eye chilli

1 unwaxed lemon

½ teaspoon fennel seeds

2 cloves of garlic, peeled and halved

extra virgin olive oil, to cover

Pesto

Everyone is familiar with this classic Italian basil sauce. Pesto couldn't be easier to make and when it's homemade it's a thing of beauty – a stunning vibrant green colour with a taste of pure summer. Give a little jar of this sauce that's loaded with fresh basil, pine nuts and pecorino with a box of fresh tortellini (page 88) and snappy grissini sticks (page 87).

MAKES 2 SMALL JARS

75g basil leaves

2–3 fat cloves of garlic, roughly chopped

75g pine nuts

250ml fruity olive oil

75g finely grated Pecorino cheese

salt and freshly ground black pepper

Put the basil, garlic and pine nuts into the bowl of a food processor. Blend the ingredients until they are roughly chopped, then add almost all the olive oil and blend again until finely chopped and combined. Mix in the grated Pecorino, taste and add salt and freshly ground black pepper.

Spoon the pesto into small sterilised jars (see page 168). Pour a little olive oil over the top and seal. Label and store in the fridge until you are ready to give it as a present.

Pesto will keep, in the fridge, for up to 1 week.

Pickled Vegetables for Pâté and Picnics

An absolute must for serving alongside pork Rillettes (page 64) or any pâté or terrine which might need something sharp and crunchy to cut through the richness.

Prepare the vegetables the day before you want to bottle the pickles, as they need to brine overnight in the salt.

Top and tail the courgette, cut in half lengthways and cut into 1cm thick slices or dice. Deseed the pepper and cut into 1cm thick chunks or strips. Top and tail the French beans and cut into 2cm lengths. Peel the carrot and cut into pieces the same size as the courgette. Peel the onions and cut into small wedges through the root. Tip all the vegetables into a plastic or ceramic bowl, toss with the sea salt, cover and leave overnight.

The next day, rinse the vegetables under cold running water and pat dry on kitchen paper.

Put the vinegar into a pan with the spices, bay leaf and garlic. Bring to the boil, then reduce the heat and simmer very gently for 5 minutes so that the spices can infuse into the vinegar.

Spoon the vegetables into a sterilised jar (see page 168), add the tarragon and pour over the hot vinegar, ensuring that all of the vegetables are completely covered. Seal the jar immediately and leave to cool completely before labelling. Store for 1 month before opening.

Store for months unopened in a cool, dark cupboard or larder. Once opened, store in the fridge and use within 2 months.

MAKES 1 LARGE JAR

1 courgette

1 red pepper

1 handful of French or runner beans

1 medium carrot

2 small onions

1 tablespoon sea salt

800ml white wine vinegar

1 teaspoon yellow mustard seeds

½ teaspoon black peppercorns

4 allspice berries

½ teaspoon coriander seeds

1 bay leaf

2 cloves of garlic, peeled and halved

2 sprigs of fresh tarragon

Ginger and Lemongrass Cooler

Serve this refreshing summer cordial diluted to taste with soda or sparkling mineral water and plenty of ice as a twist on ginger beer.

MAKES ABOUT 1 LITRE

500g golden caster sugar
pared zest and juice of
1 unwaxed lemon
3 sticks of lemongrass
125g peeled fresh ginger
1 teaspoon citric acid

Place the sugar, lemon zest and juice with 1 litre of water in a large saucepan. Cut the lemongrass stalks in half, give them a good bash with a rolling pin to bruise the stems and add to the pan.

Whiz the peeled ginger in a food processor until finely chopped. Add to the pan and bring the mixture slowly to the boil. Reduce to a very gentle simmer and continue to cook for a further 20 minutes. Remove the pan from the heat and leave the syrup to one side for about 4 hours, to allow the ginger and lemongrass to impart maximum flavour.

Bring the syrup to the boil again, add the citric acid and stir to dissolve. Strain the syrup through a fine sieve or a piece of muslin, then pour into sterilised bottles (see page 168), using a funnel, and seal. Label the bottles when cold.

Serve diluted to taste with soda or sparkling mineral water and plenty of ice. It will keep in the fridge for up to 1 month.

Pork Rillettes

Rillettes are a type of rustic paté where pork belly is cooked very slowly with plenty of seasoning and herbs until meltingly tender, it's then shredded before being packed into jars and sealed with a layer of fat. Spoon rillettes onto rustic bread and serve with Pickled Vegetables (page 62).

Preheat the oven to 150°C/300°F/gas mark 2. Cut the pork belly into 2cm pieces and place in a large bowl. Dice the streaky bacon and add to the bowl.

Lightly crush the juniper berries and peppercorns in a pestle and mortar and add to the bowl along with the mace, garlic, thyme and bay leaf. Season well with sea salt and black pepper.

Pour over the white wine, mix well, then transfer to a large solid casserole or terrine dish and cover with a tight-fitting lid. Cook on the bottom shelf of the preheated oven for 3–3½ hours, or until the pork is completely tender and falling apart, and stirring once or twice during the cooking time.

Remove from the oven and pour the meat into a colander set over a bowl. Discard the thyme, bay leaf, peppercorns and juniper berries. Put the drained meat into another bowl, then pull it into shreds, using 2 forks. Taste for seasoning, adding more salt and pepper if needed. Pack the meat into sterilised jars (see page 168), or a terrine or earthenware dish, and pour over a little of the liquid that drained into the bowl.

When the meat is cool, cover and chill for 30 minutes. Pour over a layer of the strained fat or goose fat, seal the jars and chill until ready to serve.

Stored in the fridge, rillettes will keep for a couple of weeks provided the meat is covered with a good layer of fat. Bring back to room temperature to serve.

MAKES 3 X 450g JARS

1.5kg boned and skinned pork belly

4 rashers of streaky smoked bacon, rind removed

6 juniper berries

6 black peppercorns

1 blade of mace

5 fat cloves of garlic, peeled and sliced

2 large sprigs of fresh thyme

1 bay leaf

sea salt and freshly ground black pepper

300ml dry white wine

2–4 tablespoons goose fat (optional)

AUTUMN

CHAPTER 3

Apricot and Almond Brownies

These brownies are definitely for grown ups – they are rich, dense and deeply fudgy. Give them as a thank-you gift for dinner in place of a store-bought box of chocolates. Cut into small squares they are delicious with coffee, tea or just about anything.

Preheat the oven to 170°C/325°F/gas mark 3. Grease and line the base of a square 23cm baking tin with non-stick baking parchment.

Warm the Marsala or brandy in a small pan, add the chopped apricots and leave to soak for 10 minutes.

Toast the almonds for 5 minutes in a baking tray in the preheated oven, then leave to cool and roughly chop.

Melt the butter and chocolate together either in a bowl set over a pan of barely simmering water or in the microwave on a low setting. Stir until smooth and leave to cool slightly.

Whisk the eggs and sugar in a bowl, add the vanilla and whisk into the melted chocolate. Sift the flour and fold into the mixture along with the chopped almonds and soaked apricots. Pour into the prepared tin and bake on the middle shelf of the oven for 25 minutes until the top has formed a crust but the underneath is still soft. Cool in the tin, then cut into squares.

Stored in an airtight container, they will keep for 2–3 days.

MAKES ABOUT 16 BROWNIES

2–3 tablespoons Marsala or brandy

125g dried apricots, roughly chopped

150g blanched almonds

150g unsalted butter, diced

225g plain chocolate (72% cocoa solids), chopped

4 large eggs

300g soft light brown or light muscovado sugar

1 teaspoon vanilla extract

125g plain flour

Honeycomb

Honeycomb and chocolate – the perfect combination for bonfire parties or camping trips.

Line a 20cm square baking tin with lightly oiled foil. Half fill the sink with cold water and have ready a whisk and the bicarbonate of soda.

Tip the sugar, syrup, cream of tartar and vinegar into a medium-sized, solid-based pan. Add 5 tablespoons water and set the pan over a medium heat. Stir until the sugar has dissolved, then bring the mixture to the boil. Continue to cook until the mixture turns amber-coloured and reaches 'hard crack' stage, or 154°C/300°F on a sugar thermometer.

As soon as the caramel reaches the right temperature, remove the pan from the heat and plunge into the sink of cold water to speed up the cooling process. Working quickly, tip the bicarbonate into the caramel and whisk to combine evenly; the mixture will foam up like a mini volcano. Pour into the prepared tin in an even layer and leave to cool.

Melt the chocolate in a bowl set over a pan of barely simmering water and stir until smooth. Remove from the heat and cool slightly. Turn the honeycomb out of the tin, peel off the foil and break into chunks. Half dip each piece into the melted chocolate. Leave to harden before packaging.

Stored in an airtight container, it will keep for 2–3 days.

MAKES ABOUT 20 PIECES

300g caster sugar

150g golden syrup

pinch of cream of tartar

1 teaspoon white wine vinegar

1½ teaspoons bicarbonate of soda

150g dark or milk chocolate

Chocolate and Hazelnut Spread

A grown-up version of a childhood favourite, this is delicious when spread thickly onto toast, inbetween cake layers or when sandwiched in the middle of cookies – or if no-one's looking straight from the jar with a big spoon...

Preheat the oven to 180°C/350°F/gas mark 4. Tip the hazelnuts on to a baking sheet and toast in the preheated oven for about 5–7 minutes, until pale golden. Remove the nuts from the oven and cool slightly. Tip the warm hazelnuts into a food processor and chop until they become an almost smooth paste.

Gently melt the chocolate, condensed milk and hazelnut oil in a small pan over a low heat. Stir until smooth and add to the hazelnut paste in the food processor. Add a pinch of salt and blend, then add the hot water and blend again until the mixture has a thick, spreadable consistency.

Spoon into a pretty sterilised jar (see page 168) and leave to cool. Cover with a lid and label when cold.

It will keep in the fridge for up to 2 weeks.

MAKES 1 X 450g JAR

75g blanched hazelnuts
100g dark chocolate (72% cocoa solids), chopped
100ml condensed milk
1–2 tablespoons hazelnut oil
pinch of salt
3–4 tablespoons hot water

English Muffins

Muffins make an irresistible afternoon tea when split in half, toasted and spread with lashings of butter and homemade cherry jam or chocolate spread (see pages 49 and 72). They'd be just perfect after a bracing walk in the autumn chill or toasted over an open fire on a Sunday afternoon.

Heat the milk in a large saucepan until it is warm to the touch, then add the sugar and yeast and stir well. Leave to one side for about 5 minutes, until the yeast has formed a thick, foamy crust on top of the milk.

Tip the flour and salt into the bowl of a free-standing mixer fitted with a dough hook. Pour the milk mixture into the flour and knead on medium speed for about 5–7 minutes, until the dough is silky and smooth but not wet.

Turn the dough out on to a work surface lightly dusted with flour and knead briefly by hand to bring it into a neat ball. Place in a large, clean bowl, cover with clingfilm and leave in a warm, draught-free place for around 1 hour, or until the dough has doubled in size.

Lightly dust the work surface and a large baking sheet with a little more flour. Turn the dough on to the work surface and knead again for 1 minute, then roll out to a thickness of just over 1 cm. Using a plain round 7–8 cm cutter, stamp out muffins from the dough and place well apart on the floured baking sheet. Re-roll the dough scraps and stamp out more muffins. You should end up with about 8–10 muffins in total.

Cover loosely with oiled clingfilm, and set aside for another 30–40 minutes to rise again until doubled in height.

Heat a griddle pan or solid-based frying pan over a medium heat and cook the muffins in batches over a low heat for 5–7 minutes on each side, until well risen and golden brown.

They will keep for 2–3 days if well wrapped in foil. I would package them wrapped in a pretty cloth or in a basket.

MAKES 8–10 MUFFINS

- 325ml full-fat milk
- 2 teaspoons caster sugar
- 1½ teaspoons active dried yeast
- 500g strong plain white flour, plus extra for dusting
- 1 teaspoon sea salt

Anzac Biscuits

MAKES ABOUT 20 BISCUITS

125g plain flour
100g desiccated coconut
100g rolled oats
75g soft light brown sugar
pinch of salt
125g unsalted butter
2 tablespoons golden syrup
½ teaspoon bicarbonate of soda
2 tablespoons boiling water

One theory surrounding the origin of these oat biscuits is that they were baked by the wives and families of soldiers from Australia and New Zealand who were fighting in the trenches in World War one. They were packaged into tins and sent by ship to the troops in food parcels. Nowadays they are a popular homemade biscuit and are often made for fundraising on ANZAC day on 25th April.

Preheat the oven to 180°C/350°F/gas mark 4 and line 2 baking sheets with non-stick baking parchment.

In a large mixing bowl stir together the flour, coconut, oats, sugar and salt.

Melt the unsalted butter and golden syrup together in a small pan set over a low heat, or in the microwave on a low to medium setting. Stir until smooth.

In a small bowl mix together the bicarbonate of soda and boiling water. Add to the dry ingredients along with the melted butter and golden syrup, and stir until smooth.

Roll level tablespoons of the mixture into rough balls in your hands and arrange on the prepared baking sheets, leaving plenty of space between them. Flatten them slightly with your hands and bake on the middle shelf of the preheated oven for about 15 minutes, until golden brown. Cool the cookies on the trays and package into pretty boxes or bags once completely cold.

These will keep for up to 1 week in an airtight box (although they were originally made to be kept for weeks on long sea journeys to the troops).

Sea-salted Caramels

You really do need a sugar thermometer for making caramels and toffees, but it won't be a wasted investment – once you've tried these caramels you'll be hooked. The saltiness is just enough to cut through the intense caramel sweetness, making them dangerously moreish. Wrap each caramel in a twist of non-stick baking parchment.

Grease a 15–17cm square tin with sunflower oil. Place the caster sugar in a deep pan with 2 tablespoons of cold water. Set the pan over a medium heat until the sugar has dissolved, then bring to the boil and continue to cook until the sugar has turned to a deep amber-coloured caramel. Remove the pan from the heat and immediately add the remaining ingredients and stir until smooth.

Return the pan to the heat and bring back to the boil. Continue to cook until the caramel reaches 130°C/250°F on a sugar thermometer. Remove from the heat, leave to settle for 30 seconds, then pour into the prepared tin and leave until cold before turning out of the tin and breaking into pieces.

These will keep for 4–5 days in an airtight box or wrapped in non-stick paper in a jar.

MAKES ABOUT 20 CARAMELS

150g caster sugar
150g light muscovado sugar
100g unsalted butter
200ml double cream
3 tablespoons golden syrup
1 teaspoon sea salt flakes

Peanut or Macadamia Brittle

Use shelled, unsalted macadamia nuts or peanuts for this old-fashioned candy recipe. break the cooled brittle into chunky pieces and package into bags or boxes lined with waxed paper.

Although delicious eaten just as it is, brittle would be delicious broken into small pieces and scattered over ice cream or a fudgy, frosted chocolate cake.

MAKES ABOUT 20 PIECES

- sunflower oil, for greasing
- 75g soft light brown sugar
- 200g caster sugar
- 75g golden syrup
- 25g unsalted butter
- ½ teaspoon bicarbonate of soda
- pinch of salt
- 175g shelled and skinned peanuts or macadamia nuts

Grease a solid baking sheet with sunflower oil.

Tip both sugars and the golden syrup into a medium-sized heavy pan. Add 75ml water and stir over a medium heat until the sugar has completely dissolved. Add the butter and stir until melted.

Bring the mixture to the boil and continue to cook steadily until the temperature reaches 154°C/310°F on a sugar thermometer.

Remove from the heat and immediately add the bicarbonate of soda, salt and nuts, stirring well as the mixture foams up. Pour on to the baking sheet and spread level with the back of a wooden spoon.

Once the brittle is completely cold and hardened, break it into pieces and package in cellophane bags.

It will keep for 3–4 days in an airtight box.

Creamy Vanilla Fudge with Chocolate and Nuts

It might be creamy, but this fudge is a little bit richer and more decadent than normal with the addition of dark chocolate and toasted nuts. You could also try adding some rum-soaked raisins or brandy-infused dried morello cherries in place of the nuts.

Line the base and sides of a 15cm square baking tin with a sheet of foil lightly greased with sunflower oil.

Place the caster sugar in a medium-sized, solid-based pan. Add the evaporated milk, full cream milk and a pinch of salt and set the pan over a medium heat to slowly and evenly dissolve the sugar, stirring gently from time to time. Once the sugar has completely dissolved, increase the heat slightly and bring to a gentle boil.

Clamp a candy thermometer on the side of the pan, and stirring occasionally to prevent the sugar catching on the bottom of the pan, continue to cook the fudge at a gentle boil until it reaches the 'soft ball' stage or 115°C/240°F.

Immediately remove the pan from the heat and set it on a heatproof surface. Stir in the butter and vanilla extract and leave the fudge to cool in the pan for 2–3 minutes. Once the fudge has cooled slightly, beat it vigorously with a wooden spoon for about 5 minutes until the fudge thickens and starts to lose its glossy sheen. Add the chopped chocolate and almonds and stir until combined. Spoon the fudge into the prepared tin and spread level with a spatula.

Leave to cool completely then cut into squares and package into bags or boxes lined with waxed paper.

This will keep for 1 week if well wrapped and stored in an air tight container.

MAKES ABOUT 20 SQUARES

sunflower oil, for greasing
500g caster sugar
50g unsalted butter
170ml can evaporated milk
125ml full cream milk
large pinch of salt
2 teaspoons vanilla extract
75g dark chocolate, chopped
50g chopped toasted almonds, hazelnuts or pistachios

Ginger Snapdragon Cookies

Decorate the top of each of these extra gingery cookies with a small square of fine edible gold leaf which is available in small books from sugarcraft or baking suppliers.

Preheat the oven to 180°C/350°F/gas mark 4 and line 2 solid baking sheets with non-stick baking parchment.

Cream together the softened butter and caster sugar until light and fluffy. Add the golden syrup, treacle and beaten egg and mix until smooth. Sift together the dry ingredients and stir into the mixture. Add the chopped stem ginger and mix again until thoroughly combined.

Using 2 spoons, place walnut-sized balls of the mixture on the prepared baking sheets, spacing them well apart to allow enough space for them to spread during cooking. Bake in batches on the middle shelf of the preheated oven for about 10–12 minutes, or until the cookies are golden brown – the edges should be crisp and the middle still slightly soft. Cool completely before packaging.

Stored in an airtight box or biscuit tin, these will keep for 4–5 days.

MAKES ABOUT 20 LARGE COOKIES

200g unsalted butter, softened
125g caster sugar
175g golden syrup
75g black treacle
1 large egg, beaten
425g self-raising flour
1 teaspoon bicarbonate of soda
4–5 teaspoons ground ginger
large pinch of cayenne pepper
pinch of salt
2 nuggets of stem ginger, finely chopped

Slow-roasted Tomatoes

The long, slow cooking of these tomatoes capture the smell and taste of summer – then semi-preserves it in a jar. Using home-grown tomatoes would make this gift even more special. Try to use ripe, flavoursome tomatoes, and nothing too large, as they will take much longer to cook. The cooking time will vary anyway, depending on the size of tomatoes used. Serve with bread and cheese, in a salad, or even in a pasta sauce.

Preheat the oven to 120°C/250°F/gas mark ½.

Drizzle a large, shallow roasting tin with the olive oil. Cut the tomatoes into quarters and arrange in the tin, cut side uppermost. Sprinkle with the caster sugar, oregano and garlic. Scatter the thyme over the top, season with salt and pepper and drizzle with more olive oil.

Cook the tomatoes on the middle shelf of the preheated oven for around 3–5 hours, depending on the size of the tomatoes, until the skins have wrinkled and the tomato flesh has dried out. Turn the tray round a couple of times during the cooking so that the tomatoes cook evenly. You may need to start checking them after 4 hours, removing any smaller ones that are cooking quicker than the rest.

Pack the roasted tomatoes into a sterilised jar (see page 168) with some fresh basil leaves. Pour over extra virgin oil to cover and seal the jar.

They will keep for up to 1 week in the fridge.

**MAKES ABOUT 24
(2 X SMALL JARS)**

2–3 tablespoons olive oil, plus extra for drizzling

10–12 smallish ripe tomatoes

1 teaspoon caster sugar

1 teaspoon dried oregano

3 cloves of garlic, peeled and sliced

2 sprigs of fresh thyme

1 teaspoon sea salt

sea salt and freshly ground black pepper

500ml extra virgin olive oil

fresh basil leaves

Duck Confit

Duck confit will keep for weeks in a large glass jar so long as the meat is well covered in goose fat and the jar unopened, making it a perfect gift to include in a housewarming hamper. The duck legs are first cured in salt, spices and herbs and then cooked very slowly in goose fat until the meat is meltingly tender.

Arrange the duck legs in a single layer in a large ceramic or glass dish.

Put the garlic, salt, peppercorns and juniper berries into a mortar and pound with a pestle until the peppercorns and juniper berries are very lightly crushed. Tear the bay leaves into small pieces and strip the leaves from the thyme sprig, then add to the mortar and stir well. Using your hands, rub the salt mixture all over the duck legs. Cover and chill for 24 hours, turning the legs over in the salt after 12 hours.

Preheat the oven to 150°C/300°F/gas mark 2. Very quickly rinse the duck legs under cold water to remove the excess salt, then pat them dry on kitchen paper and lay them in a roasting tin or ovenproof dish that will hold them snugly. Warm the goose fat over a low heat and pour over the duck legs – they should be completely covered. Put the roasting tin on the hob, over a low heat, until the fat reaches simmering point, then transfer to the middle shelf of the preheated oven and cook for about 2 hours, until the meat is meltingly tender. You may need to turn the legs in the fat to ensure that they cook evenly.

Remove from the oven and leave to cool, then transfer the legs to a large sterilised kilner jar (see page 168), pour over the goose fat so that they are completely covered, seal and store in the fridge until needed. Attach a label with the reheating instructions:

Preheat the oven to 220°C/425°F/gas mark 7. Remove the duck legs from the container and scrape off almost all the goose fat. Roast skin side down on a solid baking sheet for 10 minutes, then drain off any excess fat. Turn the legs over and continue to cook for a further 10–15 minutes, until golden and crisp.

Make sure to attach a label with instructions for reheating and serving which should include a recipe for crispy sautéed potatoes, cooked in goose fat of course.

SERVES 6

- 6 duck legs
- 4 fat cloves of garlic, peeled and sliced
- 6 rounded tablespoons coarse sea salt
- 1 teaspoon black peppercorns
- 2 juniper berries
- 2–3 bay leaves
- 1 large sprig of fresh thyme
- 3 x 340g cans of goose fat

Tomato Chutney

No cheese sandwich is complete without a good dollop of chutney and this one packs a punch with a couple of red chillies and some generous spices. It would be a suitable rival to barbecue sauce for hamburgers or other grilled meats.

MAKES ABOUT 4 JARS

1.25kg ripe tomatoes

2 onions

1 red pepper

1 Bramley apple

2 large red chillies, deseeded and finely chopped

2 fat cloves of garlic, crushed

3cm piece of fresh ginger, grated

1 teaspoon black peppercorns

8 allspice berries

4 cardamom pods, bruised

500ml white wine vinegar or cider vinegar

1 fresh bay leaf

350g soft light brown sugar

2 teaspoons black mustard seeds

salt and freshly ground black pepper

Using a small knife, make a cross on the bottom of each tomato. Place in a bowl, cover with boiling water, leave for 30 seconds to 1 minute to loosen the skins, then drain and refresh under running cold water. Peel the tomatoes and roughly chop the flesh. Peel and finely chop the onions. Deseed and dice the pepper. Peel, core and dice the apple.

Put the chopped tomatoes, onions and apples into a preserving pan. Add the chillies, garlic and ginger. Wrap the peppercorns, allspice berries and cardamom pods in a small square of muslin, tie securely with kitchen string and tie the end of the string to the pan handle so that the spices are submerged in the vegetables.

Pour over the vinegar, add the bay leaf and bring to the boil, then reduce the heat and simmer gently for about 25–30 minutes, until the vegetables are tender. Add the sugar and stir to dissolve. Increase the heat slightly and simmer steadily until the chutney has reduced to a thick consistency. Add the mustard seeds and season with salt and freshly ground black pepper.

Remove the bay leaf and the muslin spice bag, then spoon the chutney into warm sterilised jars (see page 168) and seal immediately. Allow to cool completely before labelling and storing.

Leave the chutney to mature for at least 4 weeks after bottling and before using. Once opened it should be stored in the fridge and used within 1 month.

Grissini really are a doddle to make and with a hint of fennel seed and chilli they are delicious to snack on or serve with dips.

Wrap a bundle of grissini sticks in a twist of greaseproof paper and give with a jar of Pesto (page 61) or Roasted Tomato Passata (page 90).

Fennel Seed, Chilli and Parmesan Grissini

MAKES ABOUT 25–30 GRISSINI

375g strong white bread flour, plus extra for dusting

3 teaspoons fast-action dried yeast

1 teaspoon sea salt

1 teaspoon fennel seeds, crushed

¼ teaspoon crushed dried chillies

200–250ml milk

3 tablespoons olive oil

4 tablespoons finely grated Parmesan cheese

Tip the flour, yeast, salt, fennel seeds and chillies into a large mixing bowl and make a well in the middle.

Warm the milk and pour it into the bowl along with the olive oil. Mix with a wooden spoon until the dough comes together. Add the Parmesan and mix until incorporated.

Lightly dust a work surface with a little flour, then turn the dough out of the bowl and knead for about 5 minutes until smooth. Shape it into a ball and return the dough to the bowl. Cover with clingfilm and leave in a warm, draught-free place for about 1 hour until the dough has doubled in size.

Turn the dough out of the bowl and knead very lightly for 1 minute. Lightly dust the work surface again with flour and roll the dough out into a rectangle with a thickness of around 5–7mm. Using a long sharp knife, cut the dough into strips just under 1cm wide. Using your hands, quickly roll the strips one at a time to make them slightly more rounded and a little longer. Arrange on baking sheets, leaving space between the grissini.

Leave to rise again for another 15–20 minutes while you preheat the oven to 180°C/350°F/gas mark 4. Cook the grissini sticks in batches on the middle shelf of the preheated oven for 10–12 minutes, until crisp and golden brown. Leave until completely cold before packaging.

Stored in an airtight container, these will keep for 4–5 days.

Tortellini with Roasted Butternut Squash, Spinach and Ricotta

Preheat the oven to 180°C/350°F/gas mark 4 and line a medium-sized roasting tin with foil. Tip the squash into the roasting tin and add the whole, unpeeled garlic. Drizzle with olive oil and season well with salt and freshly ground black pepper. Roast on the middle shelf of the preheated oven for about 40–45 minutes, until the squash is tender.

Meanwhile cook the spinach. Tip the leaves into a sauté pan with a splash of water and cook over a medium heat for a couple of minutes, until wilted. Tip into a sieve, and when cool enough to handle squeeze out any excess moisture with your hands. Finely chop the spinach and mix in a bowl with the ricotta, Pecorino and sage.

Remove the cooked squash from the oven and allow to cool slightly. Squeeze the garlic from its skins and blend in a food processor with the squash until smooth. Add to the spinach and cheese mixture, mix well and season with salt and freshly ground black pepper. Set aside.

To make the pasta, tip the flour into the bowl of a food processor, then add the beaten eggs and a pinch of salt. Pulse the mixture until it comes together into a ball – you may need to add a couple of teaspoons of cold water. Turn the dough out on to a lightly floured work surface and knead until smooth. Flatten into a disc, wrap in clingfilm and chill for at least 30 minutes.

Lightly dust the work surface with flour and roll out the pasta dough until it is about 1mm thick. Using a plain round cookie cutter with a diameter of about 9cm, stamp out discs from the dough. Gather up the scraps, knead into a ball, re-roll and stamp out more pasta discs. Arrange the discs on the work surface and spoon 1 rounded teaspoonful of filling into the top half of each. Lightly brush the edges with cold water, then fold over into a semi-circle and press to seal. Bring the points of the semi-circle together and pinch.

Pack the fresh pasta in single layers into a box lined with waxed or greaseproof paper. Cover and label with the cooking instructions.

Cook in a large pan of boiling salted water for 2–3 minutes or until tender. Drain and toss with the very best extra virgin olive oil, homemade pesto or passata and a good scattering of freshly grated parmesan. These will keep for about 4 days if covered in the fridge.

Making these little tortellini is far easier than you'd imagine, so receiving a box of these little pasta parcels is a gift that most people would be impressed by. You don't need a pasta machine here but do try to roll the pasta as thin as possible before stamping out the shapes.

Package into a shallow box lined with parchment and serve with a small jar of Pesto (page 61).

SERVES 4

1 medium-sized butternut squash, peeled and cut into large chunks

4 cloves of garlic

1–2 tablespoons olive oil

100g young leaf spinach

2 tablespoons ricotta cheese

2 tablespoons grated Pecorino cheese

2 teaspoons chopped fresh sage

300g pasta flour, plus extra for dusting

3 large eggs, lightly beaten

salt and freshly ground black pepper

Passata

If you grow your own tomatoes then making homemade passata is the perfect way to use up an abundance of your crop. It's almost like bottling a little bit of summer that you can use throughout the year. Why not package a bottle of passata with a box of homemade tortellini (see page 88) and a bundle of grissini (see page 87) to give as a housewarming gift or to the lover of all things Italian?

Preheat the oven to 180°C/350°F/gas mark 4.

Halve the tomatoes and put into a large roasting tin. Peel the onions and cut into wedges. Trim and slice the celery, and peel and roughly chop the carrot. Add everything to the tin along with the unpeeled garlic cloves. Quarter and de-seed the red peppers and also add to the tin.

Drizzle with the oil and vinegar and add the oregano sprig. Sprinkle over the sugar and chilli and season well with salt and freshly ground black pepper. Cover loosely with kitchen foil and roast on the middle shelf of the oven for about 45 minutes, or until the vegetables are tender.

Remove the tray from the oven and pop the garlic cloves from their skins. Peel the skin from the red peppers and discard the oregano. Tip the roasted vegetables into a food processor and blend until smooth. Taste and check the seasoning, adding more salt and pepper or a pinch of sugar if needed. Add the chopped fresh basil and pour the hot passata into clean, sterilised jars (see page 168). Leave to cool before labelling.

Passata will keep for 2–3 months if unopened. Once opened, store in the fridge and use within 3–4 days.

MAKES 2–3 LARGE JARS

1.5kg ripe tomatoes

2 small onions

1 stick of celery

1 medium carrot

1 whole head of garlic

2 red peppers

6 tablespoons extra virgin olive oil

splash of balsamic vinegar

1 bushy sprig of fresh oregano

3 teaspoons caster sugar

pinch of crushed dried chilli

2 tablespoons chopped fresh basil

salt and freshly ground black pepper

Pickled Shallots

You will need to prepare these pickled shallots at least a month before you plan on giving them away, to allow the delicious spiced vinegar to work its magic.

MAKES 2 LARGE JAM JARS

500g small shallots or pickling onions

50g sea salt

500ml white wine vinegar

1 rounded tablespoon light muscovado sugar

1 bay leaf

4 allspice berries

pinch of crushed dried chilli flakes

½ teaspoon coriander seeds

½ teaspoon mustard seeds

4 black peppercorns

Peel the shallots, leaving them whole and the root end attached. The easiest way to do this is to tip the shallots into a bowl, cover with boiling water and leave them for 2–3 minutes to soften the skins. Then drain and peel them, using a small sharp knife. Dissolve the sea salt in 500ml water in a ceramic bowl, add the peeled shallots, cover and leave to soak for 24 hours.

While the shallots are soaking, prepare the spiced vinegar. Pour the vinegar into a stainless steel pan, add the sugar and spices and place the pan over a medium heat, stirring occasionally until the sugar has dissolved. Slowly bring to the boil, then reduce the heat and simmer very gently for 10 minutes. Remove from the heat and leave the vinegar to cool.

Drain the shallots, rinse well in cold water and pat dry on kitchen paper.

Pack the shallots into sterilised jars (see page 168) and pour over the spiced vinegar, making sure that the shallots are completely covered. Seal the jars and label.

This is definitely one for the boys! Serve as part of a ploughman's lunch with man-sized hunks of crusty bread and a wedge of tangy hard cheese. Store in a cool, dark place for at least 1 month before opening. Once opened, use within 1 month.

Pickled Beetroot

Banish all thoughts of over-vinegary pickled beetroot here. These wedges of beetroot are packed into a slightly sweet and spiced vinegar. Squirrel the jars away in a cool cupboard until Christmas when they'd be perfect to take to any Boxing Day lunch to eat with cold cuts of meat.

This is another great recipe that's ideal for allotment holders when faced with an unexpectedly large crop of beetroot.

Wash the beetroots and put them into a pan. Cover with cold water and add the salt. Bring to the boil, then reduce the heat and cook at a gentle simmer until the beetroots are tender when tested with the point of a small sharp knife.

While the beetroots are cooking, prepare the spiced vinegar. Put both vinegars into a pan with the sugar, cinnamon, star anise, coriander, mustard seeds and peppercorns. Set over a low to medium heat until the sugar has dissolved, then bring slowly to the boil. Simmer for 2–3 minutes and remove from the heat.

When the beetroots are cooked, drain them and set aside until cool enough to handle. Peel off the skins and cut each beetroot into 6 or 8 wedges through the root. Reheat the spiced vinegar until just boiling. Add the beetroot, shallots and garlic, simmer for 1 minute, then remove from the heat.

Using a slotted spoon, remove the beetroot wedges from the liquid and pack into the sterilised jars (see page 168). Pour over the spiced vinegar to cover the beets and immediately seal. Leave to cool before labelling.

Store for months unopened in a cool, dry cupboard or larder. Once opened, store in the fridge and use within 1 month.

MAKES 2 LARGE JAM JARS

500g whole beetroots (approx. 4 medium beetroots)

1 teaspoon sea salt

300ml malt vinegar

75ml balsamic vinegar

75g light muscovado or soft light brown sugar

1 cinnamon stick

2 star anise

1 teaspoon coriander seeds

1 teaspoon mustard seeds

4–5 black peppercorns

2 small shallots or 1 large, peeled and sliced

2 cloves of garlic, peeled and sliced

Damson or Plum Cheese

'Cheese' is a bit of a misnomer here. This is really a damson paste that is quite delicious when served with cheese in much the same way as Membrillo (or quince paste) is traditionally eaten with Manchego cheese.

MAKES ABOUT 4 SMALL JARS

1kg damsons
approx. 750g caster sugar
juice of ¼–½ a lemon

Rinse the damsons under cold running water and place in a large pan with 150ml of water. Cover and cook over a low heat until the fruit is very tender, and the flesh has come away from the stones and cooked down to a thick pulp. Remove the pan from the heat and push the damsons through a nylon sieve into a clean bowl.

Scoop the purée into a measuring jug and make a note of the amount. For every 600ml of damson purée you will need 450g of caster sugar and a small squeeze of lemon juice.

Put the damson purée, the correct weight of sugar and the lemon juice into a solid-bottomed sauté pan or saucepan and set over a low to medium heat. Cook the mixture very gently at first to dissolve the sugar, then continue to cook, stirring regularly, until it becomes a thick paste — it should have the consistency of lightly whipped cream.

Pour the damson cheese into small, straight-sided sterilised jars (see page 168) and seal immediately. Label the jars once completely cold.

Store for months unopened in a cool, dark cupboard or larder. Once opened, store in the fridge well wrapped in clingfilm and use within 1 month.

Damson or Plum Vodka

After you have strained off the damsons from the vodka the resulting fruit could be added to a boozy crumble if you're feeling brave!

Rinse the damsons under cold running water. Prick each damson 4 or 5 times with a fork and place them in a sterilised (see page 168), wide-necked preserving jar with a capacity of 2 litres.

Add the caster sugar, cinnamon stick and lemon zest and pour over the vodka. Secure the lid and give the jar a good shake to dissolve the sugar. Leave in a cool, dry, dark place for at least 3 months, shaking the jar at least once a week or every time you walk past.

After 3 months the vodka will be a deep plum colour and deeply flavoured by the damsons. Taste and add more sugar if desired. Strain the vodka through a colander into a large bowl. Strain again, either through muslin or paper coffee filters, into sterilised bottles (see page 168). Seal the bottles with sterilised stoppers and attach labels.

This never lasts for long in my house, but will keep for ever in reality.

MAKES 1 X 70cl BOTTLE

500g damsons
125g caster sugar
1 cinnamon stick
pared zest of 1 unwaxed lemon
1 x 70cl bottle of good-quality vodka

WINTER

CHAPTER 4

Cheese Sablés

Buttery, crumbly, cheesey, just a little spicy and absolutely perfect with a glass of chilled white wine. Coat the outside of these biscuits with a mixture of sesame and kalonji seeds to make them a more sophisticated cocktail nibble.

Tip the flour, salt, cayenne, mustard powder, cumin or caraway seeds and some black pepper into the bowl of a food processor. Add the diced butter and use the pulse button to rub it into the dry ingredients. Add the grated cheeses and pulse again until the dough just comes together – you may need to add a drop of cold water.

Tip the dough out on to a lightly floured work surface and roll into a log roughly 5cm in diameter, wrap in clingfilm and chill in the fridge for a couple of hours or until firm.

Preheat the oven to 180°C/350°F/gas mark 4 and line a baking sheet with non-stick baking parchment. Take the log out of the fridge, remove the clingfilm and brush with milk before coating in the sesame and kalonji seeds (if using). Slice the log into discs, roughly 5mm thick, and arrange on the baking sheets, spacing the biscuits well apart.

Bake on the middle shelf of the preheated oven for 12–15 minutes, or until crisp and golden. Once completely cold, the sablés can be packaged.

Stored in an airtight box, they will keep for 4–5 days.

MAKES ABOUT 24

175g plain flour, plus extra for dusting

1 teaspoon sea salt

½ teaspoon cayenne pepper

½ teaspoon dry mustard powder

1 teaspoon cumin or caraway seeds, lightly crushed

150g unsalted butter, chilled and diced

75g finely grated mature Cheddar cheese

75g finely grated Parmesan cheese

1 tablespoon milk

sesame seeds (optional)

kalonji (black onion) seeds (optional)

freshly ground black pepper

Wholegrain Honey Mustard

This recipe is incredibly easy to make, but will of course be influenced by the quality of the ingredients you use.
I have suggested using white wine vinegar, but you could look out for specialist vinegars using specific grape varieties.

Mix the mustard seeds, chilli flakes, vinegar and cinnamon together in a bowl. Cover and set aside for at least 12 hours and up to 24.

Remove and discard the cinnamon stick from the mustard seeds, add the honey and mix well. Transfer three-quarters of the mixture to either a food processor and blend until lightly crushed or pound the mustard using a pestle and mortar.

Combine with the remaining soaked mustard seeds and season with salt. Spoon into sterilised jars (see page 168), cover and seal before labelling.

 Store for months unopened in a cool, dry cupboard or larder. Once opened, it will keep for 2–3 months at least in the fridge.

MAKES 3 JARS

225g mixed yellow and brown mustard seeds

1 teaspoon crushed dried chilli flakes

275ml white wine vinegar or cider vinegar

1 cinnamon stick

4 tablespoons clear honey

1 teaspoon sea salt

This mustard is perfect when served with all manner of cold meats, in sandwiches or quite simply with homemade oatmeal biscuits (see page 120) and marinated goat's cheese (see page 58).

Limoncello

This tipple is like a little ray of boozy citrus sunshine at the end of a heavy meal and should be served very cold, in little shot glasses. If you're lucky enough to find some lemons with stalks and leaves attached, these would make a very beautiful label or gift tag.

Wash and dry the lemons and remove the zest in fine strips, using a vegetable peeler. Squeeze the juice from the lemons and set aside. Pour 100ml of water into a small pan, add the zest and sugar and bring slowly to the boil, stirring occasionally until the sugar has dissolved. Reduce the heat and simmer very gently for 15 minutes. Add the lemon juice and simmer for a further 5 minutes. Remove from the heat and set aside to cool.

Pour the vodka into a large sterilised preserving or kilner jar (see page 168) and add the lemony syrup. Secure the lid and give it all a good shake. Set aside in a cool, dry, dark place for a week, shaking the jar every day. Strain off the lemon zest and decant the limoncello into a pretty bottle.

This will keep for months.

MAKES 1 X 70cl BOTTLE

6 unwaxed lemons
250g caster sugar
1 x 70cl bottle of good-quality vodka

Chocolate Truffles

You may need to make up two batches of these truffles – one to give away and one to keep for yourself. I have given a number of flavour options that can be added to the basic recipe, but if you prefer you could simply add a couple of tablespoons of your favourite liqueur. The rolled truffles are coated in crisp dark chocolate but are just as delicious when simply dusted with cocoa.

Line a baking tray with non-stick baking parchment.

Put the cream, sugar and salt into a pan over a medium heat. Bring to the boil, stirring to dissolve the sugar, then reduce the heat and simmer very gently for 1 minute. Put the chopped chocolate in a bowl. Remove the pan from the heat and pour the mixture over the chocolate. Stir until the chocolate has melted and the mixture is smooth.

Divide the mixture evenly between 2 bowls and add whichever flavour you have chosen (see below). Mix thoroughly, then leave to cool and set in the fridge for about 2 hours.

Scoop 1 teaspoonful of set truffle mixture into the palm of your hand. Roll it quickly into a ball and place on the lined baking tray. Repeat with the remaining mixture. Chill the truffles until firm.

To temper the chocolate for coating the truffles, place 100g of the finely chopped chocolate in a small bowl set over a pan of barely simmering water. The bottom of the bowl should not come into contact with the water or the chocolate may scorch. Stir the chocolate until melted and smooth. Remove the bowl from the pan and add the remaining 50g of chopped chocolate. Stir until melted and thoroughly combined and the chocolate has cooled and thickened slightly. Return the bowl to the pan and warm the tempered chocolate over the water once more. It is now ready to use.

First lay out a clean sheet of baking parchment. Taking 1 truffle at a time, drop it into the tempered chocolate. Using a fork and working quickly, roll the truffle to coat it in the chocolate, then lift it and allow the excess to drip back into the bowl, tapping the tines of the fork on the edge. Carefully slide the truffle off the fork on to the clean baking parchment. Repeat with the remaining truffles and leave to harden before packaging into pretty boxes.

Stored in a cool place, truffles will keep up to one week. If kept in the fridge, bring them out 30 minutes before serving.

MAKES ABOUT 35 TRUFFLES

TRUFFLES:

200ml double cream

75g light muscovado sugar

pinch of sea salt

250g best-quality dark chocolate, finely chopped

TO COAT:

150g best-quality dark chocolate, finely chopped

FLAVOUR VARIATIONS

CANDIED ORANGE

25g candied orange peel, finely chopped

STEM GINGER

25g stem ginger in syrup, drained and finely chopped

CHERRY AND COCONUT

25g desiccated coconut, lightly toasted

50g dried morello cherries, chopped

Mango Chutney with Chilli and Ginger

A perfect accompaniment for any Indian meal with a stack of freshly cooked poppadums and warm naan bread. Or equally good on a picnic spooned onto crusty bread with some tangy cheese.

Place the onions, garlic, chilli and ginger in a preserving pan. Cut the apple and mangoes into 1cm chunks and add to the pan.

Crack the cardamom pods using a pestle and mortar, extract the seeds and discard the green husks. Toast the cardamom, fenugreek, cumin and coriander seeds in a dry frying pan until toasted and fragrant and lightly grind in the pestle and mortar. Toast the mustard seeds in the same frying pan and add to the preserving pan along with the lightly ground spices, cinnamon stick and ground turmeric.

Add the vinegar, black onion seeds and salt and bring slowly to the boil. Continue to cook over a medium heat until the apple and mango is pulpy, stirring from time to time. Add both sugars and continue to cook for about 30 minutes until the mixture has thickened, reduced and the fruit is very soft but still chunky.

Add the lime juice to give the chutney a little extra pep, stir to combine and remove the pan from the heat. Remove the cinnamon stick, spoon into sterilised jars (see page 168) and seal immediately.

Once the chutney is completely cold, label the jars and store in a cool, dark place for 4 weeks before serving.

Store for months, unopened, in a cool, dark cupboard or larder. Once opened, store in the fridge and use within 1 month.

MAKES 4 X 450g JARS

2 onions, peeled and finely chopped

3 fat cloves of garlic, peeled and finely chopped

1 red chilli, deseeded and finely chopped

4cm piece of fresh ginger, peeled and finely grated

1 Bramley apple, peeled, cored and quartered

juice of 1 lime

4 large ripe mangoes, peeled and stoned

4 cardamom pods

1 teaspoon fenugreek seeds

1 teaspoon cumin seeds

½ teaspoon coriander seeds

2 teaspoons black mustard seeds

1 cinnamon stick

½ teaspoon ground turmeric

350ml white wine vinegar

200g soft light brown sugar

200g golden granulated sugar

1 teaspoon kalonji (black onion) seeds

1 teaspoon salt

Spiced Cranberry Jelly

This jelly makes a delicious alternative to cranberry sauce and would be a welcome addition to any Christmas or Thanksgiving hamper.

MAKES 3–4 SMALL JAM JARS

1kg fresh cranberries

2 oranges

1 cinnamon stick

5 whole cloves

2 star anise

approx. 500g granulated sugar

Place the cranberries in a preserving pan or large saucepan. Remove the zest from the oranges using a vegetable peeler and add to the pan with the squeezed orange juice, the cinnamon stick, cloves and star anise. Add 400ml water, then cover the pan and set over a medium heat to simmer gently for 20–30 minutes until the cranberries are very tender and have burst.

Remove from the heat and pour the contents of the pan through a jelly bag suspended over a large bowl or pan. Leave the cranberries to drip through the bag for at least 4 hours or overnight, but do not be tempted to stir or push them through or the resulting jelly will be cloudy.

The next day, pour the strained cranberry juice into a measuring jug and make a note of the quantity. For every 600ml of juice you will need 450g of granulated sugar. Return the juice to a clean pan, then add the sugar and stir over a low heat until it has dissolved. Increase the heat and boil steadily until setting point is reached (see page 168).

Pour the jelly into sterilised jars (see page 168) and seal immediately. Label the jars once the jelly is completely cold.

 Store for months, unopened, in a cool, dark cupboard or larder. Once opened, store in the fridge and use within 1 month.

Piccalilli

Piccalilli is one of those old-fashioned types of pickles that I think no picnic or camping trip should be without. It's packed full of crisp vegetables that are all bound together in a bright, turmeric mustard yellow sauce and is the perfect partner to pork pies, cold cuts and doorstop cheese sarnies.

Prepare the vegetables, and try to cut them into similar-sized pieces. Cut the cauliflower into small florets. Peel the carrots and cut into thick batons or chunks. Top and tail the French and runner beans and cut into 2cm lengths. Cut the cucumber in half lengthways and scoop out the seeds. Cut the cucumber and courgette into chunks. Peel the onions.

Put all the vegetables into a large ceramic or plastic bowl. Dissolve the salt in 1.2 litres of cold water and pour over the prepared vegetables. Cover and leave overnight in a cool place.

Put the vinegar, bay leaf, mustard seeds, peppercorns, coriander seeds, allspice berries and whole garlic cloves into a large non-reactive pan. Bring to the boil, then reduce the heat and simmer very gently for 5–10 minutes. Remove from the heat and leave to cool – this will allow the seasonings to infuse into the vinegar.

In a bowl mix together the flour, mustard powder, turmeric and ginger. Add 2–3 tablespoons of the spiced vinegar and mix to a paste. Strain in the remaining vinegar and pour back into the pan. Add the sugar and bring to the boil, stirring constantly until thickened slightly. The sauce should be glossy and thick enough to coat the back of a spoon.

Drain the vegetables, rinse briefly under cold water and pat dry on kitchen paper. Add to the hot vinegar mixture and cook over a low heat for 4–5 minutes, until just tender. Spoon into hot sterilised jars (see page 168) and cover immediately. Once cold, label and store in a cool dark cupboard for about 3 weeks before using.

 Store for months, unopened, in a cool, dark cupboard or larder. Once opened, store in the fridge and use within 1 month.

MAKES 3 X 450G JARS

1 small cauliflower

2 medium carrots

125g French beans

125g runner beans

½ a cucumber

1 courgette

10 silverskin onions

75g Maldon salt

600ml white malt vinegar

1 bay leaf

2 teaspoons yellow mustard seeds

8 black peppercorns

½ teaspoon coriander seeds

3 allspice berries

2 cloves of garlic, peeled

25g plain flour

1 tablespoon English mustard powder

2 teaspoons ground turmeric

1 teaspoon ground ginger

75g caster sugar

Chocolate-coated Candied Almonds

One batch of these almonds will make enough to package into more than one gift. Although they are delicious when simply candied with their coating of sugar and cinnamon, once they are dipped in dark chocolate and given a light dusting of cocoa they become something else altogether. Package the almonds into screw-top jars tied with ribbons.

Preheat the oven to 150°C/300°F/gas mark 2 and line a medium-sized baking tray with non-stick baking parchment.

Combine the sugar, cinnamon, salt and almonds in a bowl. In a second bowl whisk the egg white until foamy. Add the vanilla extract, then the almond and sugar mixture, and stir to evenly coat the nuts.

Tip out on to the baking tray and spread in an even layer. Bake on the middle shelf of the oven for about 30 minutes, until crisp, turning the nuts a couple of times. Remove from the oven and leave to cool on the tray.

Once completely cold, you can coat the nuts in chocolate and cocoa. Break the chocolate into pieces and melt it in a heatproof bowl set over a pan of barely simmering water or in the microwave on a low setting. Stir until smooth and leave to cool slightly. Taking a few almonds at a time, dip them into the chocolate, allowing any excess to drip back into the bowl.

Leave the chocolate-coated almonds to set on the baking parchment, then dust them with cocoa and package them into boxes or bags

These will keep for about 2 weeks in a jar or airtight box.

MAKES 2 JAM JARS

100g golden caster sugar

2 teaspoons ground cinnamon

pinch of salt

200g whole almonds

1 medium egg white

1 teaspoon vanilla extract

200g dark chocolate

1–2 tablespoons cocoa, for dusting

Florentines

A box of delicate jewelled Florentine biscuits dipped in white and dark chocolate would be a sophisticated and moreish box of goodies to give to any hostess.

Preheat the oven to 180°C/350°F/gas mark 4 and line 2 solid baking sheets with non-stick baking parchment.

Finely chop the candied peel and quarter the glacé cherries. Chop the blanched almonds or pistachios. Mix the fruit and nuts together in a medium-sized bowl and set aside.

Melt the butter, caster sugar and honey in a small pan over a low heat, stirring constantly to prevent the sugar catching on the bottom of the pan. Remove from the heat and add the flour, ground ginger and salt. Stir until smooth, then add the cream and stir again. Pour on to the fruit and nuts and stir well to combine.

Spoon rounded teaspoons of the mixture on to the prepared baking sheets, leaving plenty of space between the mounds. Bake on the middle shelf of the preheated oven for about 10 minutes, or until the edges of the Florentines are golden brown. Remove from the oven and leave to cool on the baking sheets until crisp.

Melt the chocolates separately in heatproof bowls over pans of barely simmering water. Spread the underside of each Florentine with either dark or white chocolate and leave until the chocolate has hardened before packaging in single layers between sheets of waxed or non-stick paper.

Florentines will keep for 4–5 days in an airtight box.

MAKES 24 FLORENTINES

75g mixed candied peel
75g glacé cherries
75g blanched almonds
25g unsalted pistachios or flaked almonds
25g unsalted butter
50g caster sugar
1 tablespoon clear honey
25g plain flour
pinch of ground ginger
pinch of salt
2 tablespoons double cream
100g dark chocolate
100g white chocolate

Biscotti with Almonds and Figs

Biscotti are so easy to make and take no time at all to prepare.
Tie up bundles of biscotti with beautiful ribbons and package with
a set of vintage espresso cups or perhaps a bottle of Vin Santo.

Preheat the oven to 180°C/350°F/gas mark 4. Melt the butter in the microwave or in a small pan and cool slightly.

Sieve the flour, sugar, salt and baking powder into a large mixing bowl. Add the chopped almonds, figs and lemon zest and mix well with a wooden spoon.

In a small bowl whisk together the whole egg, egg yolk, vanilla extract and cooled melted butter. Make a well in the middle of the dry ingredients and pour the egg and butter mixture into it. Stir until the ingredients are thoroughly combined and come together into a ball.

Divide the biscotti dough into two equal pieces. Very lightly dust a work surface with a little plain flour and roll the dough into 2 logs, each about 20cm long. Cover a baking sheet with baking parchment and place the logs on the paper, leaving plenty of space between them.

Bake on the middle shelf of the preheated oven for about 35–40 minutes, until golden brown and firm to the touch. Remove from the oven and leave to cool on the baking tray. Turn the oven off.

When the logs are completely cold, preheat the oven to 170°C/325°F/gas mark 3 and cover 2 baking sheets with non-stick baking parchment. Using a long, sharp knife, slice the biscotti logs on the diagonal into slices no thicker than 1cm thick and arrange in a single layer on the baking sheets.

Bake on the middle shelf of the oven for about 20 minutes, until crisp. You may need to swap the trays around and turn the biscotti over halfway through cooking. Cool and package into cellophane bags or pretty boxes.

Stored in an airtight container, these will keep for about a week.

MAKES ABOUT 24

50g unsalted butter

225g plain flour, plus a little extra for rolling

150g caster sugar

pinch of salt

½ teaspoon baking powder

75g whole almonds, roughly chopped

100g dried figs (or dried morello cherries), roughly chopped

finely grated zest of ½ an unwaxed lemon

1 large egg

1 large egg yolk

1 teaspoon vanilla extract

Chocolate and Ginger Loaf Cake

I always think that if you're going to make the effort to bake a cake you may as well make two while you have the oven on. That way you can spread the love and give a chocolate cake to two lucky friends. If you prefer you could swap the stem ginger for candied peel or chocolate chips.

MAKES 2 X 500g CAKES

100g dark chocolate, chopped

2 nuggets of stem ginger in syrup

100g plain flour

40g cocoa

½ teaspoon baking powder

1 teaspoon bicarbonate of soda

25g ground almonds

pinch of salt

125ml soured cream

75ml sunflower oil

2 large eggs

150g soft light brown sugar

50ml boiling water

CHOCOLATE GANACHE:

200g dark chocolate (72% cocoa solids)

75g unsalted butter

2 tablespoons double cream

Preheat the oven to 180°C/350°F/gas mark 4. Butter and line the base and ends of 2 x 500g (1lb) loaf tins with a strip of buttered baking parchment.

Melt the chocolate either in a heatproof bowl set over a pan of barely simmering water or in the microwave on a low setting. Stir until smooth and set aside. Finely chop the stem ginger.

Sift together the flour, cocoa, baking powder, bicarbonate of soda, ground almonds and salt. Mix together the soured cream and sunflower oil.

In the bowl of an electric mixer fitted with the whisk attachment, beat the eggs and sugar until they are pale and thick and the mixture will leave a ribbon trail when the beater is lifted from the mixture. Stir in the melted chocolate and chopped ginger.

Add the sifted dry ingredients, then the oil and soured cream, and fold into the cake mixture until smooth. Whisk in the boiling water, stir until smooth and divide the mixture between the prepared tins. Bake on the middle shelf of the preheated oven for 35 minutes, or until a wooden skewer inserted into the middle of the cakes comes out clean.

Cool the cakes in the tins for 10 minutes, then transfer to a wire rack until completely cold.

To make the ganache, melt together the chocolate, butter and double cream either in a heatproof bowl set over a pan of barely simmering water or in a microwave on a low setting. Stir until smooth and combined. Set aside to cool and thicken slightly.

Using a palette knife, spread the ganache over the top of each cake and leave to set before decorating with chopped nuts and stem ginger.

 Stored in an airtight container, this will keep for 4–5 days.

Spiced Nuts

Fill homemade paper cones with spoonfuls of these mixed spiced nuts. They're the perfect little package to give to the cocktail enthusiast in your life along with a bottle of the Chilli Vodka (page 167).

Preheat the oven to 180°C/350°F/gas mark 4.

Tip all the nuts and seeds into a large bowl and drizzle over the olive oil and honey. Add the salt and spices and a generous grinding of black pepper. Mix well to evenly coat the nuts in the spices. Tip the mixture out on to a large baking tray and spread level.

Roast on the middle shelf of the preheated oven for about 10 minutes, stirring the mixture regularly so that it browns evenly. When the nuts are golden, remove from the oven and allow to cool before packaging into paper cones to serve.

These nuts will keep for 3 days in an airtight box.

MAKES 8 PAPER CONES

750g mixed nuts (Brazils, walnuts, pecans, almonds, cashews, peanuts and macadamias)

50g pumpkin seeds

50g sunflower seeds

2 tablespoons olive oil

2 tablespoons clear honey

2 teaspoons sea salt flakes

2 teaspoons cumin seeds, coarsely ground

1½ teaspoons paprika

1 rounded teaspoon celery salt

freshly ground black pepper

Pecan Snowball Cookies

Dusted with a generous scattering of icing sugar
these crumbly, buttery Snowball Cookies are scrumptious
with a cup of tea for elevenses.

Preheat the oven to 150°C/325°F/gas mark 3 and line 2 baking sheets with non-stick baking parchment.

Toast the pecans in the preheated oven for 5–7 minutes. Leave to cool, then chop in a food processor until finely ground.

Cream the softened butter and icing sugar until pale, light and fluffy. Add the vanilla extract and mix again. Sift the flour, baking powder and salt into the bowl, add the ground pecans and mix until smooth and thoroughly combined. Cover the cookie dough and chill for 30 minutes to allow it to firm up.

Roll dessertspoons of the cookie dough into balls and arrange on the baking sheets, spacing them well apart. Bake in batches on the middle shelf of the preheated oven for about 15 minutes, until pale golden. Remove the cookies from the oven and cool slightly.

Dust the cookies liberally with icing sugar and package into pretty bags or boxes once completely cold.

Stored in an airtight container, cookies will keep for 5 days.

MAKES 24 COOKIES

125g pecans
150g unsalted butter, softened
100g icing sugar
1 teaspoon vanilla extract
225g plain flour
½ teaspoon baking powder
large pinch of salt
icing sugar, for dusting

SLEEPY TEA:

dried camomile
dried lemon balm
dried passiflora
dried rose buds or
petals

DE-STRESS TEA:

dried camomile
dried lemon balm
dried lime blossoms
dried passiflora
dried skullcap

Herbal Teas

Give a box of these herbal tea bags with a beautiful vintage teapot. Ready-to-fill tea bags are usually available from herbalist suppliers – fill them with your selected blend and attach a handmade label to each bag. Alternatively, present the loose tea in glass jars or tea caddies and include instructions for making a brew using a mesh strainer.

Combine equal quantities (50g in total) of each of the dried herbs in a bowl and mix well. Scoop 1 heaped teaspoon of the blend into each tea bag, tie with fine string or cotton and attach a pretty label to each bag.

Stored in an airtight box, these will keep for at least 3 months.

Oatmeal Biscuits for Cheese

These biscuits are perfect to serve with all types of cheese but are particularly delicious when served with some homemade chutney or relish too. There are many different wholegrain flours now available so play around with different types to see which you prefer. I particularly like using a flour with wheat and barley flakes, kibbled rye and assorted seeds already added.

Sift the oat bran, flour, baking powder, mustard powder, pepper and salt into a large bowl and add any bran left in the sieve. Tip into the bowl of a food processor and add the diced butter and caster sugar.

Using the pulse button, process the mixture until the butter has been rubbed into the flour. Add the milk and pulse again until the mixture comes together to form a dough. Put it on to a flour-dusted work surface and knead very lightly and just enough to bring it together. Cover with a clean cloth and set aside for 15 minutes.

Meanwhile preheat the oven to 180°C/350°F/gas mark 4 and line 2 baking trays with non-stick baking parchment.

Lightly flour the work surface again, then roll the dough slightly thicker than a pound coin and cut out shapes, using a biscuit cutter. Re-roll any trimmings. Prick the biscuits with a fork, arrange on the prepared baking trays and bake on the middle shelf of the preheated oven for about 12 minutes, or until starting to turn golden at the edges. You may need to swap the trays over halfway through cooking.

Cool the biscuits on the baking trays for 2 minutes, then transfer them to a wire cooling rack.

Stored in an airtight tin, these biscuits will keep for a couple of weeks.

MAKES 25–30 BISCUITS

50g oat bran or oatmeal

175g wholemeal flour

2 level teaspoons baking powder

1 teaspoon dried mustard powder

½ teaspoon freshly ground black pepper

1 teaspoon sea salt

100g unsalted butter, diced and chilled

2 level tablespoons golden caster sugar

3 tablespoons milk

plain flour, for rolling

Shortbreads

Here is one basic recipe that can be adapted to make a myriad of shortbread flavours. A tin of these biscuits is somehow reminiscent of childhood and the biscuit assortment box that was brought out on high days and holidays.

MAKES ABOUT 24 IN TOTAL

VANILLA SHORTBREAD:

225g unsalted butter, softened

75g icing sugar, sifted

1 teaspoon vanilla extract

225g plain flour, plus extra for rolling

pinch of salt

CHOCOLATE SHORTBREAD:

225g unsalted butter, softened

75g icing sugar, sifted

1 teaspoon vanilla extract

225g plain flour, plus extra for rolling

50g cocoa

pinch of salt

To make the shortbread dough, cream the softened butter and icing sugar until pale and light. Add the vanilla extract and mix again. Sift the flour (cocoa, if using for the chocolate shortbread) and salt, add to the mixture and beat until smooth. Flatten the dough into a disc, wrap in clingfilm and chill until firm.

Preheat the oven to 180°C/350°F/gas mark 4 and line a baking sheet with non-stick baking parchment. Lightly dust the work surface with plain flour and roll the dough out to a thickness of about 3mm. Using cookie cutters, stamp out shapes and arrange on the baking sheet.

Bake on the middle shelf of the preheated oven for around 12–15 minutes, until crisp and pale golden. Cool on the baking sheets, then package into pretty boxes or bags.

VARIATIONS

Pistachio Chocolate-dipped Shortbread
Add 75g of finely chopped unsalted, shelled pistachios to the shortbread mixture (chocolate or vanilla). Stamp out discs of shortbread and bake. Spread the baked and cooled shortbread discs with melted dark chocolate and scatter with chopped pistachios.

Stem Ginger Shortbread
Add 1 teaspoon of ground ginger and 1 finely chopped nugget of stem ginger to the basic vanilla mixture.

Lemon Shortbread
Add the finely grated zest of 1 unwaxed lemon, 1 teaspoon of lemon extract and 1 tablespoon of finely chopped candied lemon peel to the vanilla shortbread mixture in place of the vanilla extract.

Almond Shortbread
Add 75g of finely chopped or ground almonds to the chocolate or vanilla mixture.

Hazelnut Shortbread
Add 75g finely chopped or ground hazelnuts to the chocolate or vanilla mixture.

Morello Cherry Shortbread
Add chopped dried morello cherries to the vanilla or chocolate mixture.

CELEBRATIONS

CHAPTER 5

Fortune Cookies

Fill each of these cookies with a personalised message of goodwill and give them to your family and friends at New Year or any other significant event. Bake the cookies in small quantities, as you have to work very quickly to fill and shape them once they come out of the oven before the delicate mixture becomes dry, brittle and impossible to fold.

Preheat the oven to 150°C/300°F/gas mark 2 and line 2 solid baking sheets with non-stick baking parchment.

Sift together the flour, ground ginger and salt. In a medium-sized bowl, whisk the egg whites until foamy. Add the icing sugar and vanilla extract and whisk until combined. Stir in the sifted dry ingredients, then add the melted butter and mix until smooth. Set aside for 10 minutes.

Draw 2 x 10cm circles on each sheet of baking parchment and spoon 1 tablespoon of the mixture on to each circle. Using either the back of a spoon or a palette knife, spread the mixture in an even layer to fill the circles. Bake 1 sheet on the middle shelf of the preheated oven and the other on the shelf below for about 6–8 minutes, until the cookies are starting to turn golden at the edges.

Working quickly, remove one sheet of baking parchment from the oven at a time, leaving the other baking tray inside and, using a palette knife, carefully and quickly lift the cookies off the parchment. Flip the cookie over, lay your fortune message in the middle and fold the cookie over it in half. Bring the points of the cookie together to make the fortune cookie curl and leave to cool in a muffin tin (this will help them to keep their shape). Repeat with the remaining cookies.

Once you have used up all of the mixture and all of your cookies are baked and shaped, slide the muffin tin into the oven for a further minute to brown them evenly.

Leave to cool in the tins before packaging in takeaway boxes. Stored in an airtight container, they will keep for up to 3 days.

MAKES ABOUT 12

100g plain flour
pinch of ground ginger
pinch of salt
3 large egg whites
100g icing sugar
1 teaspoon vanilla extract
75g unsalted butter, melted and cooled slightly

Seville Orange and Whisky Marmalade

Seville oranges are only around for a very short season, so it makes perfect sense to make a larger batch of marmalade than you think you'll possibly have a need for. Aside from the fact that you can only make it once a year, you'll find yourself tucking it into food hampers at every opportunity.

MAKES ABOUT 8 JARS

1kg Seville oranges
2 litres cold water
1.75kg preserving sugar
250g light muscovado sugar
5 tablespoons whisky
juice of 1 lemon

Wash the oranges thoroughly in warm water and dry them with a clean tea towel. Cut them in half and press them through a citrus squeezer to extract as much juice as possible, but don't discard the pips, pithy membrane and any orange flesh. Instead tie all this up in a square of clean muslin and set it aside on a saucer while you prepare the peel.

Using a sharp knife, thinly slice the peel into strips. Place in a large ceramic bowl and cover with 2 litres of cold water. Add the muslin bag of pips and pith, then cover the bowl and leave the peel to soak for at least 12 hours and up to 24.

The next day, put the peel, soaking water and muslin bag into a preserving pan or other large pan. Bring to the boil, then reduce the heat, cover and simmer extremely gently until the peel is very tender – this can take anything up to 1½ hours, depending on how thickly you have cut the peel. Don't be tempted to rush or skimp on this step, as once the sugar is added to the marmalade the peel will not soften any further. Remove the muslin bag from the pan, set it aside until cool enough to handle, then squeeze it between your hands to extract every last drop of juice back into the pan. Pop a couple of saucers into the fridge to be used to test the marmalade for setting point.

Add both sugars to the pan with the reserved orange and lemon juice and bring slowly to the boil to dissolve the sugar. Continue to boil steadily for about 30 minutes, skimming off any scum that rises to the surface with a slotted spoon, until setting point has been reached (see page 168). This can take anything up to an hour so keep checking every 5 minutes or so.

Once setting point has been reached, add the whisky to the pan, boil for 30 seconds, then remove from the heat. Leave the marmalade to cool in the pan for 10 minutes before spooning into sterilised jars (see page 168).

 Store for months unopened in a cool, dark cupboard or larder. Once opened, store in the fridge. It will keep for 2–3 months.

Granola

This makes a fabulous gift to take for your host or hostess if you're invited away for the weekend. You can add any selection of dried fruit and nuts – try dried cranberries, cherries or blueberries, or if you prefer something more exotic, an assortment of dried tropical fruits.

Preheat the oven to 180°C/350°F/gas mark 4.

Roughly chop the almonds and pecans and tip them into a large mixing bowl. Add the oats, all the seeds and the desiccated coconut. Roughly chop the dates and apricots, add to the bowl and mix until thoroughly combined.

Heat the sunflower oil and honey in a small pan until the honey is very runny but not boiling. Pour into the oaty mixture and stir to coat evenly.

Cover a large shallow roasting tin with a sheet of baking parchment, add the granola and cook in the preheated oven for 15–20 minutes. Stir the mixture regularly to ensure that the granola browns evenly. Once it is golden and starting to crisp, remove from the oven and leave to cool completely before spooning into a storage jar. Attach a label giving serving instructions and ingredients.

MAKES ABOUT 4 JAM JARS

50g whole almonds
50g pecans
200g rolled oats
50g pumpkin seeds
25g sesame seeds
50g sunflower seeds
50g desiccated coconut
125g medjool dates, pitted
100g dried apricots
2 tablespoons sunflower oil
175g clear honey

A delicious way to start the day, serve scattered over natural yogurt and with a compote of summer berries. It will keep for 2–3 weeks in an airtight box.

Chocolate Valentine's Cakes

Forget the usual chocolates and roses for your Valentines, and instead say 'I Love You' with these chocolate heart-shaped cakes Coated with dark chocolate ganache and topped with sugar paste roses. Specialist sugarcraft suppliers will stock a variety of ready-made flowers but making your own roses is really very simple, just make them 24 hours before topping the cakes to allow them to dry.

You will need 6 x 10cm heart-shaped cake tins with a depth of 3cm.

Preheat the oven to 180°C/350°F/gas mark 4. Brush the insides of the tins with the melted butter and dust with 1 tablespoon of the plain flour, tapping out any excess.

Melt the chopped chocolate either in a heatproof bowl set over a pan of barely simmering water, or in a microwave on a low setting. Stir until smooth and set aside to cool slightly.

Cream the butter and sugar until pale, light and fluffy. Add the egg yolks and stir until combined. Add the cooled melted chocolate and stir again. Mix the remaining 2 tablespoons of plain flour with the ground almonds, freeze-dried raspberies, if using, and salt. Add to the chocolate mixture and mix thoroughly.

In a clean bowl, whisk the egg whites until they reach stiff peaks. Stir one quarter of the egg whites into the chocolate mixture to loosen and then, using a large metal spoon, fold in the remainder.

Line the base of the cake tins with baking parchment and divide the mixture between them all, then arrange on a baking sheet and bake on the middle shelf of the preheated oven for 20 minutes, until risen and firm to the touch. Leave to cool in the tins for 5 minutes, then carefully run a small palette knife around the edges and turn the cakes on to a cooling rack and leave until cold.

To make the ganache, melt together the chocolate, butter and double cream either in a heatproof bowl set over a pan of barely simmering water or in a microwave on a low setting. Stir until smooth and combined. Set aside to cool and thicken slightly. Using a palette knife, spread the ganache over the top of each cake and leave to set before decorating with sugar paste roses or fresh berries.

MAKES 6

150g unsalted butter, softened, plus 1 tablespoon, melted

3 tablespoons plain flour

200g plain chocolate, chopped

150g caster sugar

4 medium eggs, separated

75g ground almonds

2 tablespoons freeze-dried raspberry crispies (optional)

pinch of salt

sugar paste roses, to decorate (optional)

fresh berries, to decorate (optional)

CHOCOLATE GANACHE:

200g dark chocolate (72% cocoa solids)

75g unsalted butter

2 tablespoons double cream

Stored in an airtight box or cake tin, these will keep for about 4 days.

NEW BABY

Baby Shower Cakes

Preheat the oven to 180°C/350°F/gas mark 4. Butter a 20cm square cake tin and line the base with buttered baking parchment.

Cream together the softened butter and caster sugar until light and fluffy, scraping down the sides of the bowl from time to time with a rubber spatula. Gradually add the beaten eggs (and lemon extract, if using), mixing well between additions.

Sift together the flour and baking powder with a pinch of salt and fold into the creamed mixture, followed by the milk. Fold in the ground almonds, grated lemon zest and juice, stir until smooth, then spoon into the prepared tin. Spread level and bake on the middle shelf of the preheated oven for about 25 minutes, or until a skewer inserted into the middle of the cake comes out clean.

Remove from the oven and cool in the tin for 5–10 minutes before turning out on to a wire cooling rack. Once the cake is completely cold, wrap it in clingfilm until you are ready to decorate it.

Split the cake in half horizontally using a long, serrated knife. Spread the bottom layer with the lemon curd and sandwich the layers back together. Trim the sides of the cake and cut into 9 even-sized cubes.

To make the buttercream frosting, place the egg whites in a medium-sized heatproof bowl, add the sugar and set over a pan of barely simmering water. Whisk the mixture constantly until it is hot, thickens, turns very white and glossy and will hold a ribbon trail, this will take about 4–5 minutes. Quickly pour this meringue mixture into the bowl of an electric mixer and whisk for 2–3 minutes, until cold. Gradually add the softened butter, whisking well between additions. Add the lemon extract and stir to combine. Use the point of a cocktail stick to add food-colouring paste and mix until you reach the desired shade.

Tip the grated white chocolate on to a large plate. Spread the tops and sides of each little cake with a thin layer of buttercream and spread evenly with a palette knife, then dip the sides of each cake into the grated chocolate so that each one is completely covered. Fit a piping bag with a small star-shaped nozzle and fill the bag with the remaining frosting. Pipe small rosettes on top of the cakes in neat rows and finish each cake with a sugar flower. Package in a single layer in a shallow box.

MAKES 9 CAKES

CAKES:

175g unsalted butter, softened

175g caster sugar

3 large eggs, beaten

175g plain flour

1 teaspoon lemon extract (optional)

3 level teaspoons baking powder

pinch of salt

3–4 tablespoons milk, at room temperature

50g ground almonds

grated zest and juice of ½ an unwaxed lemon

FROSTING BUTTERCREAM:

2 tablespoons lemon curd

3 large egg whites

175g caster sugar

225g unsalted butter, softened

1 teaspoon lemon extract

pink, blue, yellow and mauve food-colouring pastes

300g white chocolate, coarsely grated

little sugar flowers to decorate

Stored in an airtight container, they will keep for 2–3 days.

Take a box of these little cakes to a baby shower or as a gift to celebrate the birth of a new baby. Tint the frosting pale pastel shades of yellow, blue, mauve or pink, and top with little sugar flowers in contrasting colours.

Raspberry, Lemon and Almond Friands

These little cakes are light as air but somehow rich at the same time and filled with almonds and fresh raspberries.

Preheat the oven to 180°C/350°F/gas mark 4. Butter the insides of 12 friand or muffin tins and lightly dust with a little plain flour, tapping out the excess.

Sift the flour, icing sugar, ground almonds and salt into a large bowl and make a well in the centre. In another bowl, lightly whisk the egg whites until foamy and just holding soft peaks. Tip the egg whites and melted butter into the dry ingredients with the grated lemon zest and fold the mixture together until combined, using a large metal spoon.

Divide the mixture between the prepared tins, filling them three-quarters full. Drop 4 or 5 raspberries on to each cake and scatter with the flaked almonds.

Bake on the middle shelf of the preheated oven for about 15 minutes, until well risen and golden brown. Remove from the oven and leave to rest in the tins for 2 minutes before carefully turning out on to a wire cooling rack.

Dust lightly with icing sugar before packaging.

Package in single layers in a box or vintage cake tin or individually wrap each friand in a cellophane bag. Friands are usually baked in little oval tins but you could just as easily use muffin tins or mini loaf tins. Stored in an airtight box, they will keep for about 3 days.

MAKES 10–12 FRIANDS

75g plain flour, plus extra for dusting

225g icing sugar, plus extra for dusting

100g ground almonds

pinch of salt

5 large egg whites

135g unsalted butter, melted and cooled

grated zest of 1½ unwaxed lemons

200g raspberries

50g flaked almonds

Double Dark Chocolate, Pecan and Ginger Cookies

These are very grown-up cookies, with a double hit of chocolate and just a hint of ginger. If you prefer you can swap the ginger for candied orange peel or dried cherries.

Break 200g of the chocolate into pieces and melt it with the butter, either in a heatproof bowl set over a pan of barely simmering water or in the microwave on a low setting. Stir until smooth and set aside to cool slightly. Chop the remaining chocolate into chunks.

Whisk the sugar and eggs together in a large bowl for a couple of minutes. Add the vanilla extract, then the melted chocolate and butter mixture, and stir until smooth. Sift together the flour, baking powder, cocoa and salt. Add to the cookie mixture with the chopped chocolate, pecans and stem ginger and mix until thoroughly combined. Cover with clingfilm and chill for a couple of hours, until firm.

Preheat the oven to 180°C/350°F/gas mark 4 and line 2 solid baking trays with non-stick baking parchment. Using a dessertspoon, scoop balls of the cookie mixture on to the baking trays, leaving space between them. Flatten the cookies slightly and bake in batches on the middle shelf of the preheated oven for about 12 minutes, until firm but not crisp. Remove from the oven and let the cookies cool on the trays.

Repeat with the remaining cookie dough. Cool the cookies completely before packaging.

Stored in an airtight container, they will keep for about 5 days.

MAKES ABOUT 20 COOKIES

325g dark chocolate

125g unsalted butter

200g light muscovado or soft light brown sugar

3 large eggs

1 teaspoon vanilla extract

150g plain flour

½ teaspoon baking powder

1 tablespoon cocoa

pinch of salt

100g pecans, chopped

1 rounded tablespoon finely chopped stem ginger

Preheat the oven to 180°C/350°F/gas mark 4, and line the muffin tins with pretty paper cases.

Melt the chopped chocolate in a heatproof bowl, either over a pan of barely simmering water or in the microwave on a low setting. Stir until smooth and remove from the heat.

In the bowl of an electric mixer, cream together the softened butter and caster sugar until pale, light and fluffy. Gradually add the beaten eggs, mixing well between additions and scraping down the sides of the bowl with a rubber spatula from time to time. Add the melted chocolate and mix again until smooth.

Sift the flour, cocoa baking powder, bicarbonate of soda and salt into a bowl. Add the dry ingredients to the creamed mixture and stir in the soured cream and boiling water. Mix until smooth, then divide between the paper cases, filling each one two-thirds full. Bake on the middle shelf of the preheated oven for about 20 minutes, or until the cakes are well risen and a wooden skewer inserted into the middle comes out clean. Cool the cupcakes in the tin for 5 minutes, then transfer to a wire cooling rack and leave until completely cold before frosting.

To make the buttercream, tip the caster sugar and egg whites into a medium-sized heatproof bowl and set over a pan of simmering water without allowing the bottom of the bowl to touch the water. Whisk steadily until the mixture is thick, glossy, holds a soft peak and reaches 150°C/300°F on a sugar thermometer. Remove from the heat and scoop the mixture into the bowl of an electric mixer. Whisk for about 3–4 minutes, until cool, thick and glossy. Gradually add the softened butter, mixing well between additions. Add the vanilla extract and mix again until smooth. Fit a large piping bag with a star-shaped nozzle and fill with the buttercream. Pipe generous swirls of frosting on to the top of each cooled cupcake.

Using your hands, break up the shredded wheat and tip into a bowl. Add the melted chocolate and mix to coat thoroughly. Arrange small nests of chocolate shredded wheat on top of each cupcake, sit 4 mini eggs in each 'nest' and leave to set.

Easter Nest Cupcakes

MAKES 12–16 CUPCAKES

CAKE:

75g dark chocolate, chopped
125g unsalted butter, softened
175g caster sugar
2 large eggs, beaten
175g plain flour
1 rounded tablespoon cocoa or malted chocolate powder (Ovaltine)
½ teaspoon baking powder
1 teaspoon bicarbonate of soda
pinch of salt
125g soured cream, at room temperature
75ml boiling water

MERINGUE BUTTERCREAM:

175g caster sugar
3 large egg whites
225g unsalted butter, softened
1 teaspoon vanilla extract

DECORATION:

100g shredded wheat
150g dark chocolate, melted
chocolate mini eggs

Pack the cupcakes into pretty boxes. Stored in an airtight container, they will keep for about 5 days.

These little cakes would be just about the most perfect thing to take on an Easter egg hunt, packaged into individual boxes and tied with name tags. Look out for pretty, pastel-coloured paper cupcake cases and fancy little chocolate eggs to sit in the nests.

Doughnuts

Heat the milk until warm to the touch. Add the yeast and whisk to combine, then set aside in a warm place for about 5 minutes to activate the yeast. It is ready when the milk has a thick, yeasty foam floating on top.

Tip the flour, salt and 75g of the sugar into the bowl of a free-standing electric mixer fitted with a dough hook. Make a well in the centre and add the yeasty milk, whole egg, egg yolk and butter. Mix steadily for about 5 minutes, until the dough is smooth and elastic. It will still be slightly sticky.

Dust a work surface with a little plain flour, then scrape the dough out of the mixing bowl and knead, using your hands, for 1 minute. Shape the dough into a smooth ball and place in a large clean mixing bowl. Cover with clingfilm and leave in a warm, draught-free place for at least 1 hour, or until the dough has doubled in size.

Lightly dust the work surface with flour again and knead the dough very gently for 1 minute. Roll it out to a thickness of just over 1cm. Using a round cookie cutter, stamp out discs from the dough roughly 6–8cm in diameter. Using a smaller cutter (4–4.5cm), stamp out a smaller disc from the middle of each doughnut.

Arrange the ring doughnuts and mini round doughnuts on a lightly floured baking tray. Cover loosely with oiled clingfilm and leave to rise again for 30 minutes.

Cover a large baking sheet with a triple thickness of kitchen paper and tip the remaining caster sugar into a large bowl or shallow roasting tray. Pour the sunflower oil into a large, shallow pan (it should come halfway up the sides) and heat to 180–190°C/350–375°F.

Fry the doughnuts in small batches for about 1–2 minutes on each side, or until lightly browned. Remove from the oil with a slotted spoon and drain thoroughly on the kitchen paper before tossing in the caster sugar. Make sure the oil comes back up to temperature before frying the next batch of doughnuts.

These are best eaten on the day of making.

If you have never eaten freshly cooked, homemade doughnuts then you've missed out on something utterly delicious. Doughnuts are a common Hanukkah treat, when it is traditional to eat fried foods that symbolise the miracle of the oil that was found in the temple in Jerusalem that burned for 8 nights rather than for one.

MAKES 8 RING AND 8 MINI
ROUND DOUGHNUTS

175ml full cream milk

10g active dried yeast

450g strong white bread flour, plus extra for dusting

½ teaspoon salt

325g caster sugar

1 whole egg, beaten

1 egg yolk

75g unsalted butter, softened

plain flour, for dusting

1 litre sunflower oil, for deep frying

1 teaspoon ground cinnamon (optional)

I have made these doughnuts into rings and mini round shapes and tossed them in caster sugar after frying. When frying the doughnuts it is important to keep the oil at a constant temperature to ensure that they cook perfectly without either burning or absorbing too much oil.

JEWISH CELEBRATION
Lebkuchen

Lebkuchen are a traditional German cookie loaded with honey and spices that are baked at Christmas-time and are often elaborately decorated with royal icing. I have given a simple icing sugar glaze in this recipe but you could coat your cookies in melted dark or white chocolate instead.

MAKES ABOUT 30 BISCUITS, DEPENDING ON SIZE

3 level tablespoons clear honey

4 tablespoons black treacle

50g unsalted butter

75g dark muscovado sugar

225g self-raising flour, plus a little extra for dusting

½ teaspoon ground cinnamon

3 teaspoons ground ginger

¼ teaspoon grated nutmeg

pinch of ground cloves

pinch of ground allspice

pinch of salt

50g ground almonds

1 tablespoon finely chopped candied peel or stem ginger

finely grated zest of ½ an orange

1 large egg, lightly beaten

GLAZE:

175g icing sugar

juice of ½ a lemon

Measure the honey and treacle into a small pan. Add the butter and muscovado sugar and place over a low heat to melt. Stir until smooth, then remove from the heat and leave to cool.

In a large bowl sift together the flour, spices and salt. Add the ground almonds, the candied peel or ginger and the grated orange zest and stir to combine. Make a well in the middle of the dry ingredients and add the melted butter and honey mixture and the beaten egg. Mix well with a wooden spoon or spatula until smooth. Cover with clingfilm and chill for around 4 hours, or until firm.

Preheat the oven to 180°C/350°F/gas mark 4 and cover 2 solid baking sheets with non-stick baking parchment. Lightly dust a work surface with a little plain flour and roll out the cookie dough to a thickness of just under 1cm. Using cookie cutters, stamp out shapes and arrange on the prepared baking sheets. Bake on the middle shelf of the preheated oven for around 15 minutes, or until firm and just starting to brown at the edges.

While the cookies are baking, prepare the glaze. Sift the icing sugar into a bowl and add a dash of lemon juice and enough hot water to make a smooth glaze.

Remove the cookies from the oven and brush with a little of the glaze while still warm. Cool on wire racks, before packaging.

 Stored in an airtight box, these cookies will keep for up to 1 week.

JEWISH CELEBRATION
Rugelach

Rugelach are little crescents of tender, flakey, buttery dough not dissimilar to croissants. They are eaten throughout the year but are often made for Hannukah. In this recipe the rugelach are filled with dark chocolate and chopped pecans but are just as delicious with dried fruit and nuts.

In a mixing bowl, beat together the butter and cream cheese until smooth. Add the caster sugar and vanilla extract and mix again. Sift the plain flour and salt, add to the bowl and mix until smooth and thoroughly combined. Turn the dough out on to a floured work surface and divide into 4 even pieces. Flatten each one into a disc, wrap in clingfilm and chill for a couple of hours, or until firm.

Preheat the oven to 180°C/350°F/gas mark 4 and line 2 solid baking sheets with non-stick baking parchment.

To make the filling, finely chop the chocolate and pecans and mix with the ground cinnamon and caster sugar.

Lightly dust a work surface with a little plain flour and roll each pastry disc out into a neat circle about 2mm thick. Spread with an even layer of jam and scatter with the chocolate pecan mixture. Using a long knife or a pizza wheel, divide each circle into 6 triangles. Roll each triangle into a crescent, starting from the outside and rolling towards the point.

Arrange the pastries on the prepared baking sheets, brush with a little beaten egg and sprinkle with caster sugar. Bake 1 sheet at a time on the middle shelf of the preheated oven for around 20 minutes, until golden.

Stored in an airtight container, they will keep for about 3 days.

MAKES 24 PASTRIES

DOUGH:

225g unsalted butter, softened
225g cream cheese
75g caster sugar
1 teaspoon vanilla extract
250g plain flour, plus extra for rolling
pinch of salt

FILLING:

100g dark chocolate
100g toasted pecans
2 teaspoons ground cinnamon
75g caster sugar
4 tablespoons cherry, apricot or raspberry jam

TOPPING:

1 egg, beaten
caster sugar, for sprinkling

CHRISTMAS

Stained Glass Snowflake Cookies

I have used festive snowflake cutters for these cookies, but the same idea works just as well for almost any shape. They look beautiful hanging at a window, allowing the light to shine through the 'stained glass'. Or you could give one cookie to each guest as a place setting or table gift for the Christmas dinner table.

You will need a selection of snowflake cookie cutters.

Cream the softened butter and icing sugar together until pale and light. Add the whole egg and vanilla extract and mix again until thoroughly combined. Sift the flour with the salt, add to the bowl and mix again until smooth.

Gather the dough into a ball, flatten into a disc and wrap in clingfilm. Chill for a couple of hours, or until firm.

Meanwhile divide the boiled sweets into separate colours, place in freezer bags and crush using a rolling pin.

Preheat the oven to 180°C/350°F/gas mark 4 and line 2 solid baking sheets with non-stick baking parchment.

Lightly dust a work surface with flour and roll out the dough until it is roughly 3mm thick. Using the snowflake cutters, stamp out snowflakes in assorted sizes and arrange on the prepared baking sheets. Carefully and neatly fill the holes in the snowflakes with the crushed boiled sweets. Bake in batches on the middle shelf of the preheated oven for about 12 minutes, until the cookies are pale golden and the boiled sweets have melted and filled the holes.

Cool the cookies on the trays until hardened, and package into boxes lined with greaseproof or waxed paper once completely cold.

These will keep for 4–5 days in an airtight box.

MAKES 8–12 COOKIES

225g unsalted butter, softened
150g icing sugar
1 large egg, beaten
1 teaspoon vanilla extract
350g plain flour, plus extra for rolling
pinch of salt
assorted flavoured and coloured boiled sweets

CHRISTMAS

Date and Ginger Cake

Here's a light, gingery, fruit-filled Christmas cake that is cut into smaller cakes and then decorated to look like mini gifts.
If you prefer you could simply cover the top of each small cake with a layer of marzipan and royal icing. Stamp out icing stars to decorate and embellish with silver sugar balls or edible glitter. To finish, tie each little cake in a festive ribbon and gift tag.

Prepare the dry ingredients the day before you plan to bake the cake. Chop the dates into pieces roughly the same size as a sultana and finely chop the stem ginger. Mix the dates, stem ginger, sultanas and raisins in a large bowl with the grated lemon and orange zests and juices. Add the ginger wine, stir well, cover with clingfilm and set aside to soak and absorb the liquid overnight.

Preheat the oven to 150°C/300°F/gas mark 2 and position the shelf just below the middle of the oven. Butter a 23cm cake tin and line the base and sides with a double thickness of baking parchment.

Sift the flour, baking powder, ground ginger and mixed spice together on to a sheet of baking parchment and add the ground almonds.

In a large bowl or a free-standing mixer, cream the softened butter and both sugars together until light. Gradually add the beaten eggs, mixing well between additions. If the mixture appears curdled at any stage, add a tablespoon of the sifted flour mixture and continue to add the egg until it has all been incorporated.

Continued on next page

MAKES 1 X 23cm SQUARE OR
9 INDIVIDUAL CAKES

CAKE:

200g ready-to-eat stoned dates
4 knobs of stem ginger in syrup
175g sultanas
175g raisins
grated zest and juice of 1 un-waxed lemon
grated zest and juice of 1 orange
5 tablespoons ginger wine
250g plain flour
2½ teaspoons baking powder
3 teaspoons ground ginger
2 teaspoons mixed spice
75g ground almonds
250g unsalted butter, softened
125g light muscovado sugar
125g dark muscovado sugar
3 large eggs, beaten
3 tablespoons milk

LEMON AND GINGER SYRUP:

3 tablespoons ginger syrup, from the stem ginger jar

2 tablespoons demerara sugar

juice of ½ a lemon

juice of ½ an orange

5 tablespoons brandy or ginger wine

Using a large metal spoon or spatula, fold the sifted dry ingredients and dried fruits into the cake mix and stir until thoroughly combined. Add the milk and mix again. Spoon the cake mixture into the prepared tin(s) and spread level with the back of a spoon.

Bake in the preheated oven for about 1½ hours, loosely covering the top of the cake with a sheet of baking parchment halfway though the baking time. (This will prevent the top of the cake browning too quickly.) The cake is cooked when a skewer inserted into the middle comes out with a moist crumb.

While the cake is cooking, prepare the lemon and ginger syrup. Place all the syrup ingredients in a small pan and set over a medium heat. Bring to the boil and stir to dissolve the sugar. Simmer for about 5 minutes, until reduced by one third. Remove from the heat and leave to cool.

Leave the cake to cool in the tin on a wire rack for about 20 minutes and then turn out onto the rack and leave until completely cold. Wrap in clingfilm until ready to ice and decorate.

TO ICE THE CAKE:

6 tablespoons apricot jam
icing sugar, for dusting
500g natural marzipan
850g ready-to-roll royal icing
red food colouring paste
small silver sugar balls
ribbon

Using a large knife, trim the edges of the cake and cut into 9 even-sized cubes. Melt the jam in a small pan with a tablespoon of water. Sieve to remove any lumps and brush the jam in an even layer over the top of each cake.

Divide the marzipan into 9 even-sized pieces. Dust a clean work surface with a little icing sugar and roll each piece of marzipan out into a square, about 2–3mm thick. Carefully lay one square over a jam-covered cake and use your hands to smooth it evenly over the top and sides. Trim off any excess and repeat with the other cakes.

Cut off one quarter of the ready-made icing and tint it red using the food colouring paste. Cover with clingfilm and set aside.

Divide the white icing into 10 even-sized pieces. Lightly dust a clean work surface with icing sugar and roll 1 piece of icing out to a thickness of about 2mm. Lightly brush one of the marzipan-covered cakes with cooled, boiled water. Carefully lay the icing over the top of the cake so that it drapes over the sides. Use your hands to smooth the icing so that it covers the cake evenly. Trim off any excess and repeat with the remaining cakes.

Roll the remaining white and red icing out and cut into thin strips with a pasta wheel or large knife. Arrange the strips as ribbons over each cake and twist shorter lengths into bows. Lightly brush with a little water and use to decorate the top of the cake.

Package each cake into a festive box. Stored in an airtight container, these cakes will keep for up to 2 weeks.

Panettone

Brush the inside of an 18cm, deep-sided cake tin with sunflower oil. Tip the raisins into a small bowl, cover with boiling water and set aside for 20 minutes to plump up. Drain the raisins and dry on kitchen paper. Mix them with the candied peel and the lemon and orange zest.

Heat the milk until it is warm to the touch and add the dried yeast and 1 teaspoon of the caster sugar. Mix well and leave to one side for 5 minutes to allow the yeast to activate and form a thick foam on top of the milk.

Place 425g of the flour, the remaining caster sugar and the salt into the bowl of an electric mixer fitted with a dough hook. Make a well in the middle of the dry ingredients and add the warm milk and yeast mixture, whole egg and yolk, honey, vanilla extract and softened butter. Mix for about 5 minutes, until the dough is smooth, soft, slightly sticky and elastic. You may need to add a little more flour if the dough is too sticky.

Add the dried fruit and grated zests and mix again until well distributed throughout the dough. Turn the dough out on to a work surface, lightly dust with flour and knead for 1 minute. Shape the dough into a smooth ball and place in a large, clean bowl. Cover with clingfilm and leave in a warm, draught-free place for at least a couple of hours, or until doubled in size.

Lightly dust the work surface with a little more flour and lightly knead the dough again for 1 minute. Shape into a ball and place in the prepared tin, smooth side uppermost. Loosely cover with oiled clingfilm and leave for at least 2–4 hours, until the dough is really well risen and has at least doubled in size again. (This will take considerably longer if your kitchen is on the cool side.)

Preheat the oven to 170°C/325°F/gas mark 3. To make the egg wash, beat the egg yolk and milk together and gently brush over the top of the panettone. Using a long sharp knife or scalpel, cut a cross into the top of the loaf and leave to rise for another 10–15 minutes.

Cook the panettone in the bottom third of the preheated oven for about 45 minutes, or until well risen and golden brown. If the top is browning too quickly, turn the oven down slightly for the last 15 minutes of cooking.

Leave the panettone to cool in the tin for 5 minutes before turning out on to a wire cooling rack.

Wrapped and stored in an airtight box, it will keep for 1 week.

SERVES 8–10

sunflower oil, for brushing tin
75g raisins
50g candied peel, finely chopped
grated zest of 1 unwaxed lemon
grated zest of 1 orange
125ml milk
10g or 1 level tablespoon active dried yeast
50g caster sugar
450g strong white bread flour, plus extra for dusting
½ teaspoon salt
1 large egg, beaten
1 large egg yolk, beaten
1 tablespoon clear honey
2 teaspoons vanilla extract
75g unsalted butter, softened

EGG WASH:

1 egg yolk
1 tablespoon milk or cream

This sweet, fruity bread is traditionally eaten in Italy at Christmas time, and is delicious cut into thick slices and served for breakfast with a steaming cup of coffee. Any leftovers can be turned into a very special and indulgent bread and butter pudding. Present the whole loaf wrapped in a large sheet of cellophane and tied with a big gauzy ribbon.

CHRISTMAS
Stollen

Stollen is a Christmas spiced bread originating from Germany that's loaded with dried fruits and filled with a thick layer of marzipan.

At this time of year with numerous gifts to think about, it makes perfect sense to double up on your baking especially as you'll never be short of worthy recipients.

Place the raisins, sultanas, currants, peel and cherries in a medium-sized bowl. Add the clementine or orange zest and juice and the brandy and leave to soak for an hour or so until the fruit has absorbed almost all of the liquid. Add the chopped almonds and mix well.

Sift the flour, salt, mixed spice, ground cardamom seeds and caster sugar into the bowl of a free-standing electric mixer fitted with a dough hook. Warm the milk, add the dried yeast and stir well. Set aside for 5–10 minutes, until the yeast has formed a thick foam on top of the milk, then add to the dry ingredients with the softened butter, vanilla and the beaten egg. Knead the dough in the mixer for about 5 minutes, until smooth. Add the soaked fruit and nuts and mix again until evenly distributed throughout the dough.

Turn the dough out on to a lightly floured work surface and shape into a ball. Place in a large, clean bowl, cover with clingfilm and leave in a warm, draught-free place for at least 1 hour, or until doubled in size.

Turn the dough out on to a lightly floured work surface again and knead lightly for 1 minute. Divide into three even pieces and roll each piece out to the size of a rectangle, roughly 20 x 15cm. Divide the marzipan into 3 even pieces and roll each one into a log 15cm long. Place a marzipan log just off the middle of each piece of dough, brush the edges with a little milk, then fold the dough over the marzipan and press to seal.

Arrange the stollen on non-stick baking sheets, cover loosely with lightly oiled clingfilm and leave in a warm, draught-free place until doubled in size. Preheat the oven to 180°C/350°F/gas mark 4.

Bake the stollen, one at a time, on the middle shelf of the preheated oven for about 25 minutes, or until risen and golden brown. Cool on wire racks, then dust liberally with icing sugar before packaging into cellophane parcels tied with festive ribbon.

 Stollen will keep for a week or so if wrapped well in foil or in a tin and is delicious warmed and sliced for breakfast.

MAKES 3 LOAVES

75g raisins

75g golden sultanas

25g currants

50g candied peel, finely chopped

50g natural glacé cherries, quartered

grated zest and juice of 2 clementines or 1 orange

2 tablespoons brandy

50g blanched almonds, roughly chopped

550g strong white bread flour, plus extra for rolling

½ teaspoon salt

1 teaspoon ground mixed spice

seeds from 5 cardamom pods, ground

40g caster sugar

250ml milk

15g active dried yeast

100g unsalted butter, softened

1 teaspoon vanilla extract

1 large egg, beaten

450g marzipan

icing sugar, for dusting

Chocolate, Nut and Fig Cake

This cake makes a fantastic, indulgent alternative to the more traditional Christmas cake and would be perfect to serve in small slices at a large festive gathering.

Finely chop the figs and place them in a bowl with the brandy or Marsala. Leave to soak for a couple of hours.

Preheat the oven to 150°C/300°F/gas mark 2 and position a shelf just below the middle of the oven. Butter a 23cm springform cake tin and line the base with a disc of buttered baking parchment.

Toast the hazelnuts and almonds in the preheated oven for about 7 minutes, until pale gold in colour. Cool completely, then finely chop, either in the food processor or by hand. Add the flour, cinnamon and salt and mix to combine thoroughly.

Place the chocolate in a heatproof bowl with the diced butter. Melt the chocolate and butter either over a pan of barely simmering water, without allowing the bottom of the bowl to touch the water, or in the microwave on a low setting. Stir until smooth, then set aside to cool slightly.

Whisk together the egg yolks, caster sugar and honey until the mixture is thick, pale and will hold a ribbon trail – this is easiest in a free-standing electric mixer fitted with a whisk attachment. Add the melted chocolate mixture, the flour and nut mixture and the soaked figs and any leftover brandy and stir until smooth.

In a spotlessly clean and dry bowl, whisk the egg whites with a pinch of salt until stiff but not dry. Stir a large spoonful of the egg whites into the cake mixture to loosen it slightly, then gently fold in the remainder.

MAKES 1 X 23cm ROUND CAKE

CAKE:

125g ready-to-eat dried figs

3 tablespoons brandy or Marsala

100g blanched hazelnuts

100g blanched almonds

50g plain flour

½ teaspoon ground cinnamon

pinch of salt

350g dark chocolate (72% cocoa solids), broken up

150g unsalted butter, diced

5 large eggs, separated

75g caster sugar

4 tablespoons clear honey

ICING:

3–4 tablespoons apricot jam

icing sugar, for dusting

200g natural marzipan

200g dark chocolate (72% cocoa solids)

75g unsalted butter

2 tablespoons double cream

1 tablespoon clear honey

Spoon the mixture into the prepared tin and spread level. Bake on the middle shelf of the preheated oven for about 1 hour, or until a skewer inserted into the middle of the cake comes out with a moist crumb. Loosely cover the cake with a sheet of baking parchment for the last 15 minutes of cooking time if the top appears to be browning too quickly. Cool the cake in the tin for 20 minutes, then turn out on to a wire rack and leave until completely cold. Wrapped well in foil, the cake will keep for 2 weeks if you do not want to ice it straight away.

Once the cake is cold (or the next day), it can be iced. Place the cake on a cooling rack set over a baking tray. Melt the apricot jam over a low heat or in a microwave, and pass it through a sieve. Brush the top and sides of the cake with a thin layer of the melted jam. Lightly dust a clean work surface or board with a little icing sugar and roll the marzipan out into a large thin circle about 30cm in diameter. Carefully lay the marzipan over the cake to completely cover the top and sides in a smooth, thin layer. Trim off any excess. Brush with a little more warm jam.

Melt together the chocolate, butter, cream and honey. Stir until smooth, then remove from the heat. Set aside for about 20 minutes to cool and thicken slightly. Pour the icing on to the top of the cake and smooth it over the sides to coat evenly, using a palette knife. Leave the cake in a cool place to allow the icing to set before serving in thin slices.

Package into a large box or cake tin and, once opened, keep well wrapped.

Un-iced, the cake will keep well for a couple of weeks if wrapped in baking parchment and clingfilm. Once iced, stored in an airtight box, the cake will keep for about 1 week.

Panforte

Chock full of nuts, dried fruit and spices – panforte is delicious dusted with icing sugar, cut into small wedges or squares and served after dinner with coffee. Originally from Sienna and although not specifically a festive treat it would certainly make an ideal Christmas present. I have suggested making it into two smaller cakes so that you can make two gifts at once.

Grease 2 x 18cm round tins and line the base of each with a disc of rice paper.

Preheat the oven to 180°C/350°F/gas mark 4. Spread the almonds and hazelnuts on a baking tray and toast in the preheated oven for about 5–7 minutes until lightly golden. Cool slightly, then roughly chop with the pistachios and tip into a large bowl. Add the chopped dried fruit and mix well. In another small bowl, mix together the spices, flour, cocoa and salt. Add to the dried fruit and nuts and mix until thoroughly combined. Lower the oven temperature to 150°C/300°F/gas mark 2.

Combine the honey and sugar in a medium-sized pan and stir over a low heat until the sugar has dissolved. Bring to the boil and continue to cook until the mixture reaches 115°C/240°F on a sugar thermometer. Remove from the heat, pour into the fruit and nut mixture and mix well. Spoon into the prepared tin and spread level.

Bake on the middle shelf of the preheated oven for 45–60 minutes, until firm. Remove from the oven and cool in the tin. Run a palette knife around the edge of the tin and carefully ease out the panforte. Dust with icing sugar to serve.

Stored in an airtight container, panforte will keep for weeks.

MAKES 2 CAKES

sunflower oil, for greasing

100g blanched almonds

100g blanched hazelnuts

75g unsalted shelled pistachios

300g mixed dried fruits, including apricots, candied peel, raisins, figs and medjool dates, roughly chopped

1 teaspoon ground cinnamon

½ teaspoon ground ginger

½ teaspoon ground cloves

½ teaspoon ground nutmeg

½ teaspoon freshly ground black pepper

90g plain flour

1 rounded tablespoon cocoa

pinch of salt

175g clear honey

175g caster sugar

icing sugar, to serve

Cashew and Almond Barfi

This is my version of a popular Indian sweet that is often prepared and given during festivals and holidays. Edible silver leaf is readily available in sugarcraft shops or from online suppliers, and is usually sold in books of 10–12 small sheets.

Line a 20cm square baking tin with lightly oiled baking parchment.

Tip the cashews into a food processor and blend until finely ground. Add the ground almonds and pulse for a further 30 seconds. Mix with the caster sugar, condensed milk, full-fat milk, ground cardamom and rosewater.

Heat the clarified butter or ghee in a large non-stick frying pan and add the nut mixture. Stir constantly over a low heat for about 10–15 minutes, until the mixture thickens and comes away from the pan smoothly in a thick mass. It should be the consistency of a loose bread dough or choux pastry. Tip the mixture into the prepared tin and spread level with either a palette knife or a rubber spatula. Leave to cool for 10 minutes.

Very carefully peel one sheet of silver leaf at a time from the book and lay on the surface of the barfi to completely cover it. Leave to set completely, then cut into diamonds with a sharp knife or a pizza wheel.

Package in a single layer in a shallow box lined with waxed or non-stick baking parchment.

Stored in an airtight container, these will keep for up to 1 week.

MAKES 20–24 PIECES

200g unsalted cashews
200g ground almonds
125g caster sugar
397g can of condensed milk
75ml full-fat milk
½ teaspoon ground cardamom
1 teaspoon rosewater
2 tablespoons clarified butter or ghee
6 sheets of edible silver leaf

Wedding Cake

Making a wedding cake for someone special is perhaps the ultimate food gift. I've lost count of the number of wedding cakes that I've made for friends and family, ranging from mountains of cupcakes to variations on this particular chocolate cake.

You will need to make this cake one layer at a time.

To make the smaller cake: preheat the oven to 170°C/325°F/gas mark 3 and line the base and sides of the 20cm square tin (7–8cm deep) with a double thickness of buttered baking parchment.

Break the chocolate into chunks and place in a medium-sized heatproof bowl. Add the diced butter and melt either over a pan of barely simmering water or in a microwave on a low setting. Stir until smooth, then remove from the heat and cool slightly.

Tip the egg yolks and caster sugar into the bowl of a free-standing electric mixer and whisk until pale and doubled in volume, scraping down the sides of the bowl with a rubber spatula from time to time. Add the cooled chocolate and butter mixture and the coffee extract and stir until smooth. Fold in the ground almonds and flour, using a large metal spoon.

In another large bowl whisk the egg whites with the salt until they hold stiff peaks. Stir one third of the egg whites into the chocolate mixture to loosen it slightly, then fold in the remainder using a large metal spoon. Carefully pour the mixture into the prepared tin, spread level and bake just below the middle of the preheated oven for 1 hour and 20 minutes, or until a wooden skewer inserted into the middle of the cake comes out clean. Remove from the oven and cool the cake in the tin.

Continued on next page

MAKES 1 CAKE
(SERVES ABOUT 50 GUESTS)

SMALLER CAKE:

300g dark chocolate
200g unsalted butter, diced
6 large eggs, separated
200g caster sugar
1 teaspoon coffee extract
150g ground almonds
1 rounded tablespoon plain flour
pinch of salt

LARGER CAKE:

600g dark chocolate
400g unsalted butter, diced
12 large eggs, separated
400g caster sugar
2 teaspoons coffee extract
300g ground almonds
2 rounded tablespoons plain flour
pinch of salt

TO FINISH:

8 tablespoons apricot jam
500g dark chocolate

CHOCOLATE GANACHE:

600g dark chocolate
(72% cocoa solids)
250g unsalted butter, diced
6 tablespoons double cream

YOU WILL NEED:

1 x 20cm square cake tin
1 x 25cm square cake tin
1 x 20cm cake board
1 x 25cm cake board
dowels

To make the larger cake: butter and line the base and sides of the 25cm square cake tin with a double thickness of buttered baking parchment. Follow the method above, but use the larger quantities and cook the cake in the bottom half of the oven for about 2 hours, or until a wooden skewer inserted into the middle of the cake comes out clean. Remove from the oven and cool the cake in the tin.

When the cakes are completely cold, wrap them in clingfilm until you are ready to ice them.

When you are ready to ice the cakes, place them on the cake boards right side uppermost. Melt the apricot jam with a splash of water in a small pan and pass though a sieve to remove any lumps. Brush the top and sides of the cakes with an even coating of jam.

To make the ganache: break the chocolate into pieces and place in a heatproof bowl with the diced butter and double cream. Set the bowl over a pan of barely simmering water and stir until melted and smooth. Remove from the heat and stir the ganache well to ensure that the ingredients are thoroughly combined. Leave to cool and thicken slightly.

Cover the top and sides of each cake with the ganache, spreading it smoothly and evenly with a palette knife.

Melt the remaining chocolate and spread it in a thin, even layer over 2–3 large sheets of non-stick baking parchment. Leave in a cool place until set and then, using a large knife, cut it into strips about 2cm wide and just a little higher than the sides of the cakes. Using a palette knife, carefully lift the chocolate strips off the paper and press on to the sides of the cakes, overlapping each strip slightly.

When you are ready to finally assemble the cakes, you will first need to push some dowel into the bottom layer to ensure that it will support the weight of the top cake. Push one length of dowel into the bottom cake, right down to the cake board, and mark the height of the cake. Cut about 8 pieces of dowel the same length and push these into the cake, spacing them evenly apart. Place the large cake on the cake stand and carefully position the smaller cake on top. Decorate the cakes with a variety of small roses in your choice of colours.

The cake bases can be baked in advance and frozen un-iced, or will keep well for 3–4 days un-iced and wrapped well in clingfilm.

Small roses in varying sizes and shades make the most beautiful decoration and can be matched to the bridal flowers and colour scheme.

Beetroot-cured Gravadlax

Peel the beetroots and coarsely grate into a large bowl. Lightly crush the peppercorns, fennel seeds and juniper berries in a pestle and mortar and add to the beetroot. Add the salt, sugar, lemon zest and 2 tablespoons of the chopped dill and mix well.

Cover a large, shallow roasting tin with a triple thickness of large sheets of clingfilm. Scatter one third of the beetroot mixture on to the middle of the clingfilm and lay the salmon fillet on top, skin side down. Cover the salmon with the remaining beetroot mixture and drizzle over the vodka. Wrap the salmon tightly in clingfilm, cover with another baking tray and weigh down with a couple of cans of tomatoes or something similar. Leave the salmon to cure in the fridge for 2 days.

Before you package and serve the salmon, scrape off as much salt as possible from the fish and pat it dry with kitchen paper. Scatter with the remaining 2 tablespoons of chopped dill. Thinly slice the gravad lax, then wrap in waxed or greaseproof paper and serve with pickled cucumber slices and rye bread.

Well-wrapped in the fridge, this will keep for 4–5 days.

The salmon in this recipe is cured rather than cooked so it pays to use the very best fish that you can find. Gravad lax makes a perfect starter to a New Year's Eve party (or any celebratory dinner), or it could be served the next day when perhaps spending hours in the kitchen is not high on the agenda. Serve with the Pickled Cucumbers and a rustic loaf of rye or soda bread.

SERVES 8

3 medium-sized raw beetroots
2 teaspoons black peppercorns
2 teaspoons fennel seeds
4 juniper berries
100g coarse sea salt
75g golden granulated sugar
grated zest of 1 unwaxed lemon
4 rounded tablespoons chopped dill
1.25kg salmon fillet, scaled and pinbones removed
4 tablespoons vodka

Pickled Cucumbers

Thinly slice the cucumber and place in a colander. Scatter with the salt and mix well. Leave for 1 hour, to allow any excess moisture to drain from the cucumber.

Rinse the cucumber slices under cold running water, then pat dry on kitchen paper and place in a bowl. Whisk the remaining ingredients together, pour over the cucumber and mix well. Season with freshly ground black pepper and serve.

It will keep for 4 days in the fridge.

1 cucumber
2 teaspoons salt
2 rounded tablespoons chopped dill
2 teaspoons caster sugar
2 tablespoons white wine vinegar
1 tablespoon olive oil
2 teaspoons yellow mustard seeds
freshly ground black pepper

Brinjal Pickle

Serve this pickle with any Indian meal and alongside
Mango Chutney (page 106) and a stack of poppadums.
It's equally delicious served with any cold roast meats.

Top and tail the aubergines and cut into 2cm cubes. Place in a colander
and sprinkle with the salt. Set the colander over a bowl and leave the
aubergines to degorge (release their bitter juices) for at least 1 hour.

Place the cumin, coriander, fenugreek and fennel seeds in a dry frying
pan and toast over a medium heat. When the seeds start to give off a
lovely, toasty aroma and are just starting to brown, remove from the heat
and finely grind using a pestle and mortar. Add the cinnamon stick,
mustard seeds and turmeric and set aside.

Rinse the aubergine cubes quickly under cold water and pat dry on
kitchen paper. Heat 2 tablespoons of the sunflower oil in a large sauté
pan over a medium to high heat. Add one third of the aubergines and
fry until soft and starting to brown. Tip out of the pan and into a bowl,
and cook the remaining aubergines in batches in the same way.

Heat the remaining 2 tablespoons of sunflower oil in the pan and add the
onions, garlic, ginger, chillies and red peppers. Cook over a medium heat
for about 7–8 minutes, until soft and just starting to colour. Add all the
spices and continue to cook for a further couple of minutes. Return the
aubergines to the pan along with the tamarind paste, vinegar and sugar.
Bring to the boil, then reduce the heat to a very gentle simmer and continue
to cook for a further 30 minutes, until the pickle has thickened and the
vegetables are really tender.

Taste the pickle and add fresh lime juice and more salt if needed. Spoon
into sterilised jars (see page 168) and seal immediately. Once the pickle
is completely cold, label the jars and store in a cool dry place for at least
1 month before opening.

Store, unopened, for months in a dark, cool cupboard or
larder. Once opened and stored in the fridge, it will keep for
at least 2–3 months.

MAKES 3–4 X 450g JARS

4 medium aubergines

2 tablespoons salt

2 teaspoons cumin seeds

2 teaspoons coriander seeds

1 teaspoon fenugreek seeds

1 teaspoon fennel seeds

1 cinnamon stick

2 teaspoons black or brown
mustard seeds

2 teaspoons ground turmeric

8 tablespoons sunflower oil

1 onion, finely chopped

2 fat cloves of garlic, crushed

4cm piece of fresh ginger

2 long red or green chillies,
deseeded and finely chopped

2 red peppers, deseeded
and diced

1 rounded tablespoon
tamarind paste

300ml white malt vinegar or
white wine vinegar

5 heaped tablespoons soft light
brown sugar

juice of 1 lime

Hot Chilli Vodka for Bloody Mary

If you like a Bloody Mary to have a kick to it, then adding a measure of this fiery chilli-infused vodka is certainly one way to make it just so. You can make this as hot as you like and infuse the vodka with a selection of chillies to suit your tastes. Once the chillies have been strained off, the vodka can be stored in the freezer and served ice cold in shot glasses if you're brave.

MAKES 1 BOTTLE

6 medium-sized fresh chillies, red and green

70cl bottle premium vodka

2 sheets edible silver or gold leaf, optional

Cut the chillies in half and remove the seeds. Pour the vodka into a kilner jar, add the chillies and cover with a tight-fitting lid. Shake the vodka and leave in a cool, dry place for at least one week to allow the chillies to infuse the vodka.

Taste the vodka after one week and if it's fiery enough, strain off the chillies and decant the vodka into a clean bottle. If the vodka is not spicy enough leave it for a further week. This will depend entirely on the strength of your chillies which can vary enormously.

To make your vodka that little bit extra-special give it some sparkle with edible silver or gold leaf. Take about one cupful of the chilli vodka and pour into a blender goblet. Add a couple of sheets of silver leaf and pulse until the silver is finely chopped. Pour back into the remaining vodka, seal the bottle and label.

 Stored in the fridge, this will keep for months.

Setting Point

To test if your jam or jelly has reached setting point, drop a teaspoonful on to a cold saucer. Leave for 1 minute, then push the jam or jelly with the tip of your finger. If it wrinkles, it's ready to pour into jars. If not, continue to cook and test every couple of minutes.

Sterilising

It's important to sterilise the jars and bottles that you use for storing your food gifts as the contents will keep for far longer that way (any dirt contaminates the food inside, causing it to spoil quickly).

Sterilising is quick and easy and can be done in the oven or in the dishwasher.

Heat the oven to 180°C/350°F/gas mark 4 – don't be tempted to heat the oven any higher or you may risk the glass breaking. Lay a double layer of newspaper on each oven shelf (no need to cover the floor) and arrange the jars on top, making sure the jars are not touching. Close the oven door and heat the jars for about 20 minutes. Using thick oven gloves, remove each jar from the oven and place on a heatproof mat. Do NOT add cold food to hot jars.

Alternatively, wash clean jars in your dishwasher and, when they are ready, add hot food to the hot jars, or wait for them to cool down.

Recipes for occasions

Mother's Day

Shortbreads
Brownies
Herbal teas
Macarons
Madeleines
Nougat
Marshmallows
Raspberry or strawberry pastilles
Raspberry and rose wafers
Raspberry, lemon and almond friands
Turkish delight

Father's Day

Barbecue sauce
Brinjal chutney
Cheese sables
Cherry tomato and sweet chilli jam
Coffee and cardamon toffee
Dark chocolate and ginger cookies
Hot chilli jelly
Mango chutney
Oatmeal biscuits for cheee
Pickled shallots
Sea salted caramels
Seville orange marmalade
Sloe gin

Valentine's Day

Chocolate truffles
Valentines cakes
Fortune cookies
Lollipops
Love heart sugar cubes
Marshmallows
Raspberry and rose wafers

Easter

Easter cupcakes
Greek honey cookies

Housewarming

Biscotti
Cherry jam
Chocolate and hazlenut spread
Doughnuts
Duck confit
Fennel seed and parmesan grissini
Glogg
Granola
Hot chilli vodka
Lemon and passionfruit curd
Limoncello
Mango chutney
Tortellini with roasted squash
and spinach

Baby Shower

Baby cakes
Love heart sugar cubes
Macarons
Marshmallows
Raspberry, lemon and almond friands
Strawberry and rose cordial

Birthday

Baby cakes
Chocolate nut and fig cake
Madeleines
Turkish delight

Hen Night

Fortune cookies
Limoncello
Lollipops
Love heart sugar cubes
Macarons
Marshmallows
Raspberry and rose wafers
Summer berry vodka
Rhubarb and vanilla vodka

New Year's Day

Cheese sables
Chocolate nut and fig cake
Damson vodka
Fortune cookies
Glogg
Hot chilli vodka
Oatmeal biscuits for cheese
Panforte
Picallili
Pork rillettes
Sloe gin
Spiced nuts
Vin d'oranges

House Guest

Cordials
Candied peels
Chocolate coated candied almonds
Chocolate truffles
Creamy vanilla fudge
Damson cheese
Granola
Macarons
Nougat
Seville orange marmalade
Strawberry and vanilla conserve

Christmas

Candied peels
Duck confit
Glogg
Lebkuchen
Nougat
Panettone
Panforte
Pecan snowball cookies
Stained glass cookies
Spiced cranberry jelly
Spiced nuts
Stollen

Index

Index

Acknowledgements

I would like to say a huge thank you to all the fabulous people who were involved in the creation of this book. To everyone at Kyle Cathie, and in particular to Judith Hannam for her patience, particularly when my deadlines were looming. And also to Vicki Murrell for her attention to detail.

Thank you to Cynthia Inions for her beautiful styling with her mountains of ribbons and reams of wrapping paper. To Cath Gratwicke for her utterly beautiful photography and her infectious laughter. And to Rashna Mody Clark for pulling all the elements together so stylishly.

A huge thank you to James and Jo for their neverending support, encouragement and hospitality.

But most of all I'd like to thank my parents for instilling in me a passion for food and a love of life.

And to Mungo who can't read or cook but gives every recipe his special seal of approval.